Catching On to American Idioms

Catching On to American Idioms

Second Edition

Esther Ellin-Elmakiss

Ann Arbor

THE UNIVERSITY OF MICHIGAN PRESS

Copyright © by the University of Michigan 1993
All rights reserved
ISBN 0-472-08208-6
Library of Congress Catalog Card No. 92-63377
Published in the United States of America by
The University of Michigan Press
Manufactured in the United States of America

2001   2000   1999   1998   8   7   6   5

Preface

Because idioms are used extensively in everyday speech, it is necessary to have a good understanding of their meanings and to be able to use them properly and easily. *Catching On to American Idioms* provides the student with such experiences and the practice in usage necessary to gain needed understanding and facility.

The second edition of *Catching On to American Idioms* is divided into fifteen lessons with a review section after every five lessons. Each of the fifteen lessons is limited to twelve idioms, a comfortable number to comprehend at one time. The idioms are first used in a dialogue and then defined. These dialogues allow the student to follow David and Ana through various situations and emotions from "Moving Ahead" to "Settling Down." The definitions for each idiom are followed by a sentence that further clarifies the idiom. A variety of ample oral and written exercises in context follow. The oral exercises enable students to express themselves and to hear others. The written exercises offer them time to think about the expressions, to understand them at their own rate, and to review and/or learn grammar. A unique feature of *Catching On to American Idioms* is that most exercises, except the last two, revolve around the dialogue. This enables the student to fully comprehend and use the twelve idioms before going on to the next lesson. To facilitate self-study, an answer key is provided at the end of the text.

Even though some idioms have more than one definition, only one is focused on in each lesson. This format enables the student to grasp the idiom in that particular meaning and to feel comfortable with it. It also eliminates confusion and frustration.

Catching On to American Idioms is primarily geared toward the intermediate or advanced non-English-speaking student. It can also be very beneficial for, and easily integrated into, other forms of education in junior high schools, high schools, or universities.

Acknowledgments

Many, many thanks to Yuki Sugimoto for her excellent drawings
that depict so well the feelings of each lesson, to Dahlia Elmakiss
and Rob Rothberg for the hours of laughter and perseverance that
went into the recording of the cassettes, to Ariana Elmakiss for
her constant patience and suggestions, and to Yvette Nicola-Muha
for her commitment and tireless hours of deciphering and typing
the manuscript. Without the input and devotion of all these
people, the creation of the second edition of *Catching On
to American Idioms* would have been difficult to realize.

Contents

Moving Ahead

Ana: David, do you remember how we felt when we arrived **by air** some months ago?

David: I certainly do, Ana! I recall how **tired out** and confused we were!

Ana: Yes, but very excited, too.

David: That we were! We had marvelous visions of life in the United States, didn't we? Remember how we always discussed our dreams of **making out** well?

Ana: Yes, I do, David. We had really **counted on moving ahead** quickly, but it's just not that easy, is it?

David: That's for sure. For new arrivals like us, there are plenty of difficulties **to get through.**

Ana: Like **getting used to** the culture and **having to** correct our **broken English!**

David: And so many times of feeling **mixed up** about **which way to turn.**

Ana: Patience and hard work have been our answers, David. And **little by little** we are succeeding.

1

Definitions

by air: in an airplane, by airplane, via airplane (plane)
  They went to Washington, D.C. by air. They traveled in an airplane.

tired out: very fatigued, exhausted, overtired
  He was tired out from his trip to the mountains. He was exhausted.

to make out: to do, to manage, to handle affairs, to be successful
  She is making out well in the United States. She is doing well.

to count on: to expect to, to anticipate, to rely on
  We counted on being there by noon. We expected to be there by noon.

to move ahead: to work toward a goal, to do well, to proceed, to succeed
  He tried to move ahead at the company. He tried to get a better position.

to get through: to survive, to endure, to tolerate
  It's not easy to get through the northern winter. It's not easy to endure it.

to get used to (to be used to): to become accustomed to, to adjust to, to become familiar with
  Eventually we got used to the climate. Eventually we adjusted to it.

to have to (to have got to): must, to be required to, to be forced to
  We have to find a new place to live. We must find a new place to live.

broken English: incorrect English, poor English grammar and syntax
  They still speak broken English. Their English grammar is still incorrect.

mixed up: confused, perplexed, confounded
  I am totally mixed up when I study English. I am totally confused when I study English.

which way to turn: which choice to make, what to do, what to decide
  He didn't know which way to turn after losing his job. He didn't know what to do after losing his job.

little by little: gradually, by slow degrees
  Little by little their savings grew. Gradually, they saved more money.

None of these idioms may be separated by the object.

Exercise 1
Answer these questions from the dialogue orally.

1. When did David and Ana arrive by air?
2. Why do you think they were tired out?
3. Where did they hope to make out well?
4. What had they counted on?
5. What must David and Ana get through to move ahead?
6. What do they have to correct?
7. Why do you think David and Ana speak broken English?
8. What do they have to get used to?
9. What do you think David and Ana feel mixed up about?
10. Why wouldn't they know which way to turn?
11. What are they doing little by little?

Exercise 2
Write the idioms from the dialogue that correspond to the words in parentheses.

1. David and Ana arrived (in an airplane) _____ some months ago.

2. They were (exhausted) _____ and confused.

3. They had dreams of (managing) _____ well in the United States.

4. They had (expected to) _____ succeeding quickly.

5. (Succeeding) _____ quickly is not that easy.

6. Most new arrivals have difficult times (to endure) _____ .

7. (Adjusting to) _____ the culture can be difficult.

8. David and Ana (must) _____ improve their English.

9. They must correct their (incorrect English) _____ .

3

10. Sometimes they feel (confused) _____ about what to do.

11. They don't know (which choice to make) _____ .

12. (Gradually) _____ they are succeeding.

Exercise 3
Answer these questions orally.

1. Were you tired out after your journey to the United States? Why?
2. Did you arrive by air or by another means of transportation?
3. Did you speak broken English when you first arrived?
4. Is your English still improving little by little? How?
5. What kind of difficulties did you have to get through?
6. In what ways are you still getting used to the culture of the United States?
7. Do you feel mixed up about the reactions of people?
8. In what situations haven't you known which way to turn?
9. What helps a person to move ahead quickly?
10. How are you making out on your job? Explain.
11. What are you counting on achieving in the United States?

Exercise 4
Match the idiom to its definition by writing the letter of the definition on the line next to the idiom number.

1. _____ to have to   a. adjust to

2. _____ which way to turn   b. to survive

3. _____ mixed up   c. to succeed

4. _____ to count on   d. very fatigued

5. _____ broken English   e. via airplane

6. _____ by air   f. to anticipate

7. _____ to get through   g. gradually

8. _____ to make out   h. confused

9. _____ little by little   i. must

10. _____ tired out   j. what to do

11. _____ to get used to   k. incorrect English

12. _____ to move ahead   l. to manage

Exercise 5
Respond to these statements orally.

1. Name two items you got used to quickly in the United States.
2. Name two occasions when you were tired out.
3. Name one difficulty you had to get through.
4. Name three things you have to do daily.
5. Name two things you counted on doing in the United States.
6. Give two ways to make out well on the job.

Exercise 6
Underline the words in parentheses that best correspond to the italicized idioms.

1. He didn't know *which way to turn* when he couldn't find a job. He didn't know (what to do, how to endure it, the job location).
2. They *got through* the hot, humid summer. They (couldn't endure, tolerated, were enthusiastic about) the summer.
3. Ana was *tired out* after the trip. She was (hardly tired, a little tired, very tired).
4. David *is used to* the American culture. He is (barely aware of, unfamiliar with, accustomed to) the culture.
5. He *has to* find a job soon. He (did, must, might) find a job.
6. We *counted on* doing well. We (were confused about, were not sure about, anticipated) doing well.

5

7. We came *by air.* We came in a (taxi, boat, plane).

8. They were very *mixed up* about the system of education in the United States. They were (sure, perplexed, determined) about it.

9. She spoke *broken English.* Her English was (excellent, good, poor).

10. I hope *to move ahead* quickly on my job. I hope to (make choices, survive, do well).

11. *Little by little* his wages increase. His wages increase (slowly, rapidly, suddenly).

12. David *is making out* well on his new job. He is (surviving, successful, hardly managing).

Exercise 7
Reread the dialogue. Tell the story in your own words using the idioms.

Exercise 8
Complete the second sentence by substituting idioms for the italicized words.

1. She is *adjusting to* the new living conditions.

   She is _____ the new living conditions.

2. Correcting *incorrect English* requires time and patience.

   Correcting _____ requires time and patience.

3. They are *confused about* what to do.

   They are _____ about what to do.

4. We *proceeded* in our plans to buy a new house.

   We _____ in our plans to buy a new house.

5. He didn't know *what to do* when he lost his wallet.

   He didn't know _____ when he lost his wallet.

6. I *must* prepare my lessons for tomorrow.

   I _____ prepare my lessons for tomorrow.

7. How did you *do* at the job interview?

How did you _____ at the job interview?

8. I *anticipated* arriving at the airport one hour early.

I _____ arriving at the airport one hour
early.

9. *Gradually,* we adjusted to the different customs.

_____ we adjusted to the different customs.

10. David was *exhausted* from job hunting.

David was _____ from job hunting.

11. All luggage will go *via plane.*

All luggage will go _____ .

12. They *survived* the period of adjustment.

They _____ the period of adjustment.

Exercise 9
Change these sentences to the future tense. Use *will.*

Example: His broken English *is* difficult to understand.

His broken English ____*will be*____ difficult to
understand.

1. Little by little, he *adjusted* to the American culture.

Little by little, he _____ to the American
culture.

2. David *was* tired out from the long journey.

David _____ tired out from the long journey.

3. Her grandmother *sent* four packages by air.

Her grandmother _____ four packages by air.

4. He *had counted* on finishing the job early.

   He _____ on finishing the job early.

5. She *is moving* ahead at a rapid pace.

   She _____ ahead at a rapid pace.

6. She *makes* out well in her profession.

   She _____ out well in her profession.

7. Their broken English *improved* quickly.

   Their broken English _____ quickly.

8. They *got* used to the different customs.

   They _____ used to the different customs.

9. Do you think he*'s* mixed up?

   Do you think he _____ mixed up?

10. David *has* to attend classes for ten weeks.

    David _____ to attend classes for ten weeks.

11. They *got* through their difficulties.

    They _____ through their difficulties.

12. We *don't* know which way to turn.

    We _____ know which way to turn.

Exercise 10
Complete the idiom phrase in each sentence.

1. He was very tired _____ from working long hours.

2. When I study English grammar, I get mixed _____ .

3. She's counting _____ having a good job.

4. We have _____ learn more about shopping in the United States.

5. He moved _____ rapidly in learning English.

6. They are making _____ well.

7. We got used _____ American food.

8. We have to study a lot to improve our _____ English.

9. It's difficult to know which way _____ _____ .

10. Little _____ _____ they saved their money.

11. Will you get _____ these difficulties easily?

12. We traveled a long distance _____ air.

Exercise 11
With a partner, create and perform an interesting, funny, enjoyable dialogue. Use as many idioms from this lesson as possible.

Exercise 12
Write sentences with the idioms given.

1. tired out

_____

2. used to

_____

3. to have to

_____

4. mixed up

_____

5. broken English

_____

6. which way to turn

_____

7. to count on

_____

8. by air

_____

Exercise 13
Circle the letter of the sentence that corresponds to the idiom used in the numbered sentence.

1. Knowing which way to turn can help you succeed.
    a. Knowing your job can help you succeed.
    b. Knowing what to decide can help you succeed.
    c. Knowing many people can help you succeed.
2. He was tired out after the operation.
    a. He was excited after the operation.
    b. He was relaxed after the operation.
    c. He had no energy after the operation.
3. She was trying to move ahead in the company.
    a. She wanted a better position.
    b. She wanted a position with less responsibility.
    c. She wanted to stay in the same job.
4. All the supplies were sent by air.
    a. They were sent via boat.
    b. They were sent via plane.
    c. They were sent via subway.
5. She made out well in her second marriage.
    a. She tolerated her second marriage.
    b. Her second marriage needed improvement.
    c. Her second marriage was a success.

6. David got very mixed up driving in Boston.

   a. David got confused.

   b. David was confident.

   c. David made out well.

7. You have to have a driver's license in order to drive a car.

   a. You don't need a driver's license.

   b. You are required to have a driver's license.

   c. It is suggested that you have a driver's license.

8. Little by little, the child began to walk.

   a. Suddenly, he began to walk.

   b. Unexpectedly, he began to walk.

   c. Gradually, he began to walk.

9. She got through that terrible performance somehow.

   a. She enjoyed it.

   b. She liked it.

   c. She endured it.

10. He counted on a good job after finishing his studies.

    a. He hoped to get a good job.

    b. He expected to get a good job.

    c. He knew he would get a good job.

11. The child always used broken English.

    a. His English was good.

    b. His English was not good.

    c. His English was excellent.

12. She got used to wearing bikinis.

    a. She never wears bikinis.

    b. Wearing bikinis doesn't bother her.

    c. Wearing bikinis bothers her.

Exercise 14
Supply the appropriate preposition in each sentence. Use *in, at, to, with, from, into.*

1. I come _____ Taiwan.

2. We are going _____ the United States.

3. We intend to stay _____ my uncle.

4. Later we hope to move _____ our own home.

5. We plan to study English _____ the Adult Learning Center.

6. We will do our homework _____ the library.

7. Joe will work _____ the bakery.

8. He wants to drive _____ work.

9. We will probably shop _____ a big supermarket.

10. We hope to live _____ the United States permanently.

11. The children will ride their bicycles _____ school everyday.

12. They will arrive home _____ school at 2:30.

13. They like to play _____ the other children.

14. Sometimes they play _____ the playground.

15. They come home for supper _____ 6:00.

Lesson 2

Let's Give It All We've Got!

David: I can't wait **to get going** with my new classes at the College Extension Center.

Ana: Neither can I. Which classes did you **sign up** for?

David: I signed up for English and a computer technology course.

Ana: So did I. Do you think we can handle two courses **at the same time**?

David: Sure, why not? If we **give it all we've got,** we'll make out well **in spite of** the language barrier.

Ana: You're probably right. I definitely want **to keep up** with the class.

David: Oh, we'll keep up. All we have to do is **pay attention** to the instructors, **take notes,** and **burn the midnight oil.**

Ana: It won't be easy, but I'm counting on making out well.

David: **Take my word,** Ana. With our perseverance and determination, we'll **have it made.**

Ana: Well, we've definitely **set our sights on** a bright future, and education is one way to get there.

Definitions

to get going: to start, to begin

   When do you get going with your classes? When do you begin them?

to sign up: to register, to enroll, to join, to enlist

   I signed up for two courses. I registered for two courses.

at the same time: concurrently, simultaneously, jointly

   She will study piano and flute at the same time. She will study them simultaneously.

to give it all one's got: to try very hard, to exert much effort

   If you give it all you've got, you'll do well. If you try very hard, you'll do well.

in spite of: regardless of, although, even though

   Will he get the job in spite of his poor English? Will he get the job even though his English is poor?

to keep up (with):   to maintain the same pace as others

   Can he keep up with the class? Can he continue learning at the same pace as his classmates?

to pay attention: to listen carefully, to observe, to obey

   Pay attention to the teacher! Listen carefully!

to take notes: to write important facts from a book, a lecture, or other material

   She takes excellent notes. She writes all the necessary facts.

to burn the midnight oil: to study or work until very late into the night

   All the students burn the midnight oil during exam time. They study until very late during exam time.

to take one's word: to believe what one says without questioning

   Take my word for it, that's an excellent car. Believe me, that's an excellent car.

to have it made (to have got it made):   to get what one wants, to be lucky or fortunate

   Some people have it made! Some people get everything they want!

to set one's sights on: to intend to get or have, to want very much

   She's set her sights on being an actress. She wants to be an actress very much.

None of these idioms may be separated by the object.

Exercise 1
Answer these questions from the dialogue orally.

1. With what are David and Ana anxious to get going?
2. Where did they sign up for their courses?
3. Which two courses will they study at the same time?
4. How do you think they will give it all they've got?
5. How does David think they'll make out in spite of the language barrier?
6. How does Ana feel about keeping up with the class?
7. To whom will David and Ana have to pay attention?
8. How will taking notes and burning the midnight oil help them?
9. What does David mean when he says, "Take my word, Ana, we'll have it made"?
10. On what have David and Ana set their sights?

Exercise 2
Write the idioms from the dialogue that correspond to the words in parentheses.

1. David and Ana are anxious (to start) _____ with their new classes.

2. They have (registered) _____ for them at the College Extension Center.

3. They intend to study English and computer technology

   (simultaneously) _____ .

4. They have to (try very hard) _____ .

5. David and Ana will make out well (regardless of) _____

   _____ the language barrier.

6. Ana wants (to continue at the same pace) _____ with the class.

7. David and Ana will succeed if they (listen) _____ to the instructors.

8. They'll have to (write the facts) _____ on the lectures.

9. They'll have to (study until very late into the night) _____

_____ .

10. David says, "(Believe me) _____ , Ana, we'll do well."

11. With perseverance and determination, both David and Ana will (get

what they want) _____ .

12. They've (wanted very much) _____ a bright future.

Exercise 3
Answer these questions orally.

1. Have you set your sights on furthering your education?
2. What kind of courses would you like to sign up for?
3. How many courses would you study at the same time?
4. When could you get going with them?
5. How would you give it all you've got?
6. Do you think you could make it in spite of the language barrier?
7. How could you keep up with the class?
8. Would you be able to take notes in English?
9. Why is it important to pay attention to the instructors?
10. What might a professor ask you to take his word for?
11. Would you have to burn the midnight oil to do well?
12. How might you have it made when you finish your studies?

Exercise 4
Match the idiom to its definition by writing the letter of the definition
on the line next to the idiom number.

1. _____ to set one's sights on   a. to begin

2. _____ to have it made   b. to try very hard

3. _____ to take notes   c. to listen carefully

4. _____ to burn the midnight   d. concurrently
   oil
                                        e. to believe what one says without
5. _____ in spite of   questioning

6. _____ at the same time   f. to write important facts from
                                           lectures
7. _____ to get going
                                        g. to be fortunate
8. _____ to sign up
                                        h. to study until late into the night
9.   to take one's word
                                        i. although
10. _____ to pay attention
                                        j. to enroll
11. _____ to keep up
                                        k. to want very much
12. _____ to give it all one's got
                                        l. to maintain the same pace as
                                           others

Exercise 5
Respond to these questions orally.

1. Name one goal you have set your sights on.
2. Name two things you must get going with.
3. Name two things you can do at the same time.
4. Name one course you would like to sign up for.
5. Give two ways to keep up with the class.
6. Give one reason for burning the midnight oil.

Exercise 6
Underline the words in parentheses that best correspond to the italicized idioms.

1. He *has set his sights on* finishing his education soon. He (wants, has little desire, has no plans) to complete it soon.

2. I must *get going* with my studies if I want to succeed. I must (finish, start, terminate) them.

3. When he studies, he *gives it all he's got.* He (procrastinates, delays studying, works very hard).

4. David has learned *to take notes.* He (writes letters, writes important facts, talks too much).

5. They are doing well *in spite of* difficulties. They are doing well (because there aren't, because there are, even though there are) difficulties.

6. We *took his word* for everything. We (understood, believed, questioned) everything he said.

7. Ana *signed up* for music. She (enrolled in, observed, wrote notes in) the class.

8. Anyone can *have it made.* Anyone can (be unsuccessful, fail, get what he wants).

9. He must work and study *at the same time.* He must work and study (on alternate days, simultaneously, occasionally).

10. They often *burn the midnight oil.* They (burn oil at midnight, write important information, study until late into the night).

11. He has no difficulty in *keeping up* with the class. He is (slower than, on the same level as, better than) the class.

12. Learning is easy when you *pay attention.* Learning is easy when you (pay for your courses, listen to the instructor, attend classes).

Exercise 7
Reread the dialogue. Tell the story in your own words using the idioms.

Exercise 8
Complete the second sentence by substituting idioms for the italicized words.

1. They *get what they want* because they are ambitious.

   They _____ because they are ambitious.

2. He *began* his homework when he arrived home.

   He _____ with his homework when he arrived home.

3. They *intended to get* the best.

   They _____ the best.

4. Where do you *register* for welding?

   Where do you _____ for welding?

5. Can you take five courses *simultaneously?*

   Can you take five courses _____ ?

6. *Believe what he says,* he's a specialist.

   _____ , he's a specialist.

7. Will you do well *regardless of* the handicaps?

   Will you do well _____ the handicaps?

8. Plan *to study until very late into the night.*

   Plan _____ .

9. If you *write the important facts,* it will help tremendously.

   If you _____ , it will help tremendously.

10. It is necessary *to listen* to the instructor.

    It is necessary _____ to the instructor.

11. Can you *continue at the same pace as others?*

    Can you _____ ?

12. *Try very hard,* and you'll succeed!

    _____ , and you'll succeed!

Exercise 9
Change these sentences to the present progressive tense.

Example: They *make* out well.

They ___*are making*___ out well.

1. She *pays* careful attention in class.

   She _____ careful attention in class.

2. They *set* their sights on a bright future.

   They _____ their sights on a bright future.

3. We *will sign* up this afternoon.

   We _____ up this afternoon.

4. *Do* they *burn* the midnight oil?

   _____ they _____ the midnight oil?

5. He *hopes* to make it in spite of problems.

   He _____ to make it in spite of problems.

6. We *gave* it all we've got!

   We _____ it all we've got!

7. She *has learned* to take notes.

   She _____ to take notes.

8. We *took* her word for everything because she's the expert.

   We _____ her word for everything because she's
   the expert.

9. His friends *said* that he has it made.

   His friends _____ that he has it made.

10. He *got* going with his homework.

   He _____ going with his homework.

11. *Will* he *keep* up with them?

   _____ he _____ up with them?

12. Why *did* she *take* so many courses at the same time?

   Why _____ she _____ so many courses at the same time?

Exercise 10
Complete the idiom phrase in each sentence.

1. If we pay _____ , we might understand more.

2. He has it _____ , don't you think so? He's a very happy person.

3. I never take his _____ for anything because he lies!

4. He can't keep _____ if he doesn't listen.

5. In spite _____ his refusal to study, he still passed the course.

6. I'll give it all _____ _____ ; that's the best I can do.

7. Take good _____ ; I need to copy them.

8. Get _____ ; we are late!

9. What did you sign _____ for?

10. Why do you eat and talk _____ the same time?

11. Three nights this week I had to _____ the midnight oil.

12. What future dreams have you set your sights _____ ?

Exercise 11
With a partner, create and perform an interesting, funny, enjoyable dialogue. Use as many idioms from this lesson as possible.

Exercise 12
Write sentences with the idioms given.

1. to pay attention

   _____

2. to get going

   _____

3. to set one's sights on

   _____

4. in spite of

   _____

5. to have it made

   _____

6. to take one's word

   _____

7. to keep up

   _____

8. at the same time

   _____

Exercise 13
Circle the letter of the sentence that corresponds to the idiom used in the numbered sentence.

1. She took notes on the book she was reading.
   a. She wrote in the book.
   b. She wrote information from the book.
   c. She wrote a report about the book.

2. He has set his sights on a new automobile.
   a. He wants a new automobile.
   b. He saw a new automobile.
   c. He bought a new automobile.

3. Pay attention to the No Smoking signs.
   a. Ignore them.
   b. Obey them.
   c. Study them.

4. He couldn't keep up with them in the race.
   a. He ran too fast.
   b. He ran too slowly.
   c. He couldn't run.

5. How does she have it made?
   a. How is she doing?
   b. How is she successful?
   c. How is she feeling?

6. He signed up for the soccer team.
   a. He observed the team.
   b. He became a member of the team.
   c. He decided not to register for the team.

7. I must get going with these birthday invitations.
   a. I must finish writing the invitations.
   b. I must stop writing the invitations.
   c. I must begin writing the invitations.

8. They enjoyed their vacation in spite of the bad weather.
   a. They enjoyed their vacation because of the bad weather.
   b. They enjoyed their vacation even though the weather was bad.
   c. The bad weather spoiled their vacation.

9. He's constantly exhausted from burning the midnight oil.

    a. He studies only during the day.

    b. He rarely studies at night.

    c. He studies most of the night.

10. He took her word for it when she said she would return his money soon.

    a. He totally believed her.

    b. He felt she was lying.

    c. He knew she wouldn't return the money.

11. He was eating and talking at the same time.

    a. He was talking while he was eating.

    b. He stopped eating in order to talk.

    c. He stopped talking in order to eat.

12. She won the game because she gave it all she's got.

    a. She played fairly well.

    b. She played as well as she could.

    c. She hardly played.

Exercise 14

Supply the appropriate preposition in each sentence. Use *up, on, at, of, to, with, through, by.*

1. Let's get going _____ our plans for the trip.

2. I've set my sights _____ a safari through Africa.

3. Why should we pay attention _____ him?

4. In spite _____ their bad luck, they are still happy.

5. Where can we sign _____ for daycare?

6. Take good notes _____ his lectures and your readings.

7. Try to keep _____ with us; just walk faster.

8. The telephone and the door bell rang _____ the same time.

9. Can we count _____ you to help us?

10. It's easy to get mixed _____ when you're in a foreign country.

11. They had a lot of problems to get _____ .

12. Do you always know which way _____ turn when you're in a difficult situation?

13. Certainly, we will have _____ do the best we can.

14. He is getting used _____ his environment.

15. Little _____ little, they're enjoying the United States more.

Lesson 3

You've Got What It Takes!

David: I'm going *to make it,* Ana. That's for sure.

Ana: You will, David. *You've got what it takes.*

David: Well, I've been out there all week long *pounding the pavement, dropping off* my resumé at every office I could find.

Ana: And how do you think you made out?

David: Actually, *at first* I thought I didn't *have a chance.* There seemed to be *tons of* applicants for every job!

Ana: And then?

David: Remember that computer analyst ad I *checked out* in last night's paper? Well, I *stopped in* at the personnel office, and the manager seemed to like what I *had to offer.*

Ana: What did he say?

David: Well, all I know right now is that he's interested in me, but I'll *find out* more next week when I *go in for* an interview.

Ana: An interview? That's great, David! Just give it all you've got, and I'm sure you'll have it made!

Definitions

to make it: to attain a certain goal, to get what one wants, to be successful

> She knows she can make it. She knows she can get any job she wants.

to have got what it takes (to have what it takes):   to have the qualities or abilities to attain a certain goal

> He's got what it takes to be an actor. He has the specific qualities to be an actor.

to pound the pavement: to walk everywhere on all streets, trying to find something

> I've been pounding the pavement trying to find a job. I've been walking everywhere trying to find a job.

to drop off: to leave something at a specific place

> I'm going to drop off my resumé at the employment office. I'm going to leave my resumé at the employment office.

at first: in the beginning, at the start

> At first, he didn't understand the language. In the beginning, he didn't understand the language.

to have a chance (to have got a chance):   to have the possibility to obtain or get something

> She has an excellent chance of getting that job. She has an excellent possibility of getting that job.

tons of (a lot of):   many, a large amount

> I have tons of homework tonight! I have a large amount of homework tonight!

to check out: to observe, to look at, to read, to study

> Check out this beautiful sofa! Look at this beautiful sofa!

to stop in (to stop by):   to visit briefly, to do a short errand

> We stopped in at their home for fifteen minutes. We visited them for fifteen minutes.

to have to offer: the qualities of a person or thing

> That house has a lot to offer. That house has qualities that everyone would like.

to find out: to discover, to learn, to acquire or get information

> Where can I find out about becoming a hairdresser? Where can I get information about becoming a hairdresser?

to go in for: to attend, to be present for, to have an appointment for, to go to

He's going in for a physical examination. He has an appointment for a physical examination.

The following idioms may be separated by the object. These idioms may be said in two ways.

to drop off:

I dropped off the book at the library.

I dropped the book off at the library.

to check out:

Check out these prices.

Check these prices out.

to find out:

Let's find out the truth.

Let's find the truth out.

Exercise 1

Answer these questions from the dialogue orally.

1. Who is going to make it?
2. What does Ana mean when she tells David, "You've got what it takes"?
3. Why was David pounding the pavement dropping off resumés at every office he could find?
4. Why did David say that at first he didn't think he had a chance?
5. How many applicants are "tons of" applicants?
6. Where had David checked out one of the ads?
7. When did David stop in at the company he had checked out in the paper?
8. What do you think David has to offer?
9. What will David find out when he goes in for an interview?

Exercise 2
Write the idioms from the dialogue that correspond to the words in parentheses.

1. David is going (to get what he wants) _____ .

2. He has (the ability to reach his goals) _____ .

3. He was (walking everywhere) _____ trying to find a job.

4. David (left) _____ his resumé at every office.

5. (In the beginning) _____ he felt unsure.

6. In the beginning, he didn't think he (had the possibility) _____

    _____ of getting a job.

7. There were (many) _____ applicants!

8. David had (studied) _____ the ads the night before.

9. He (briefly visited) _____ at the place mentioned in the ad.

10. The manager liked what he (had the ability to do) _____

     _____ .

11. David said, "I'll (discover) _____ more next week."

12. I'm (attending) _____ an interview soon.

Exercise 3
Answer these questions orally.

1. How do you plan to make it in life?
2. Do you think you've got what it takes?
3. Do you think it's better to drop off resumés personally or to mail them?

4. Did you ever feel discouraged that you didn't have a chance at a particular job?

5. Have you ever pounded the pavement? For what?

6. What do you consider "tons of" applicants for one job?

7. Where do you usually check out the employment ads?

8. Do you stop in at every employment place you're interested in, or do you telephone?

9. How can you find out information about a company?

10. When you go in for an interview, do you tell them at first what you have to offer?

Exercise 4

Match the idiom to its definition by writing the letter of the definition on the line next to the idiom number.

1. _____ tons of
2. _____ to make it
3. _____ to have a chance
4. _____ to stop in
5. _____ to have what it takes
6. _____ to find out
7. _____ to go in for
8. _____ to pound the pavement
9. _____ to check out
10. _____ what one has to offer
11. _____ drop off
12. _____ at first

a. to leave something at a specific place

b. to attend

c. to have the abilities to attain a certain goal

d. to discover

e. in the beginning

f. to observe

g. the qualities of a person

h. many

i. to be successful

j. to visit briefly

k. to have the possibility to get something

l. to walk everywhere

Exercise 5
Respond to these statements orally.

1. Name two places to check out employment ads.
2. Name two places you would like to drop off resumés.
3. Name one place you have stopped in at to find out about jobs.
4. Name one position you have a chance of getting.
5. Give one reason for pounding the pavement.
6. Give one quality you have to offer.

Exercise 6
Underline the words in parentheses that best correspond to the italicized idioms.

1. *At first,* they didn't know where to go. (Sometimes, In the beginning, Finally) they didn't know where to go.
2. We decided to *stop in* at the office. We decided to (come another time, return later, visit for a short time).
3. They *pounded the pavement* for days, but couldn't find work. They (hardly walked anywhere, walked everywhere, didn't try very hard) to find work.
4. She *has a chance* of getting a promotion. She (has no hope, has no possibility, has a possibility) of getting a promotion.
5. She *has much to offer* in the field of architecture. She has (excellent qualifications, little knowledge, an excellent opportunity).
6. She *dropped off* the book at the library. She (studied, left, read) the book at the library.
7. There were *tons of* people at the concert. There were (very few, some, many) people at the concert.
8. He's *got what it takes* to succeed! He (has no desire, walks everywhere, has the qualities) to succeed!
9. He is *finding out* the truth. He is (denying, failing to find, discovering) the truth.
10. *Check out* these ads! (Read, Discard, Keep) these ads!
11. She's *going in for* an interview. She's (leaving, beginning, going to) an interview.
12. I'll *make it!* That's for sure. I'll (get what I want, do nothing, be forced to try).

Exercise 7
Reread the dialogue. Tell the story in your own words using the idioms.

Exercise 8
Complete the second sentence by substituting idioms for the italicized words.

1. Naturally, I'll *get what I want*; I'm determined to.

   Naturally, I'll _____ ; I'm determined to.

2. How did you *get that information* about it?

   How did you _____ about it?

3. He *has the qualities* to become an airline steward.

   He _____ to become an airline steward.

4. *In the beginning*, I didn't understand anything.

   _____ , I didn't understand anything.

5. Did you *read* the company's policies?

   Did you _____ the company's policies?

6. *Visit for a few minutes* before you go to work.

   _____ before you go to work.

7. *Many, many* people attended the job fair.

   _____ people attended the job fair.

8. *What qualities* does he have as a real estate broker?

   What does he _____ as a real estate broker?

9. He got this job so easily; he didn't have to *walk anywhere*.

   He got this job so easily; he didn't have to _____

   _____ .

10. She *left* a package to be mailed by UPS.

    She _____ a package to be mailed by UPS.

11. *Is there a possibility* of his getting that job?

    Does he _____ of getting that job?

12. At what time will you *attend* the interview?

    At what time will you _____ the interview?

Exercise 9
Change these sentences to the past negative form. Use a contraction.

Example: They *had* to learn about the United States.

   They ___*didn't have*___ to learn about the United States.

1. He *stops* in often in the afternoon.

   He _____ in often in the afternoon.

2. They *saw* tons of refugees on the ships.

   They _____ tons of refugees on the ships.

3. We *will go* in for an examination tomorrow.

   We _____ in for an examination yesterday.

4. At first, we *had* to buy a car.

   At first, we _____ to buy a car.

5. We *are checking out* all places for possible jobs.

   We _____ out all places for possible jobs.

6. She *had* a chance to see all her relatives.

   She _____ a chance to see all her relatives.

7. She *will be dropping* off her resumé at 9:00 a.m.

She _____ off her resumé at 9:00 a.m.

8. We *will pound* the pavement all morning.

We _____ the pavement all morning.

9. They *found* out that they would have new neighbors soon.

They _____ out that they would have new neighbors soon.

10. He *has* much to offer for that position.

He _____ much to offer for that position.

11. *Do* you *think* he has what it takes?

_____ you _____ he had what it takes?

12. *Did* he finally *make* it as a big politician?

_____ he finally _____ it as a big politician?

Exercise 10
Complete the idiom phrase in each sentence.

1. She has what it _____ , but she can't find a job.

2. _____ of people were there, so we couldn't find him.

3. That company has little to _____ ; there are no benefits and the pay is poor.

4. They found _____ everything, every little detail!

5. I'll _____ off the invitations when I visit her.

6. I'm so tired of pounding the _____ ! I need a job now.

7. _____ first he spoke broken English, but now he speaks better.

8. You have to _____ out the employment section of the newspaper very carefully.

9. Do you think I have a _____ of getting that position?

10. For sure you can _____ it! You just have to work very hard.

11. Is she going _____ for an interview soon?

12. Stop _____ on the way home from work.

Exercise 11
With a partner, create and perform an interesting, funny, enjoyable dialogue. Use as many idioms from this lesson as possible.

Exercise 12
Write sentences with the idioms given.

1. at first

_____

2. to check out (write the sentence in two ways)

_____

_____

3. to drop off (write the sentence in two ways)

_____

_____

4. tons of

_____

5. to stop in

_____

6. to have a chance

_____

7. to pound the pavement

_____

8. to go in for

_____

Exercise 13

Circle the letter of the sentence that corresponds to the idiom used in the numbered sentence.

1. He dropped off his clothes at the laundry.

    a. He left his clothes at the laundry.

    b. He ironed his clothes at the laundry.

    c. He lost his clothes at the laundry.

2. We bought tons of items at the bargain store.

    a. We bought very few items.

    b. We bought a few items.

    c. We bought a lot of items.

3. At first, the kitten was scared of everything.

    a. The kitten was always scared of everything.

    b. The kitten was scared of everything in the beginning.

    c. Later, the kitten was scared of everything.

4. We went to the park on a breezy fall afternoon to check out the foliage.

    a. We went to the park to see the foliage.

    b. We went to the park to go jogging.

    c. We went to the park because it was breezy.

5. Everyone has a chance to get a good education.

    a. Everyone has the ability to get a good education.

    b. Everyone has the possibility to get a good education.

    c. Everyone must get a good education.

6. She has what it takes to try new experiences in life.

    a. She's afraid of new experiences.

    b. She's not afraid of new experiences.

    c. She is very cautious about new experiences in life.

7. He knows he can make it as a commercial airline pilot.

   a. He has doubts about being a pilot.

   b. He is afraid of being a pilot.

   c. He is certain he can be a pilot.

8. They found out that jogging is a difficult exercise.

   a. They liked jogging because it's difficult.

   b. They discovered that jogging is not easy.

   c. They decided to begin jogging.

9. Let's stop in at Lizzy's house; I heard she's not too well.

   a. Let's visit her all afternoon.

   b. Let's visit her for 15 minutes.

   c. Let's visit her for the day.

10. You have so much to offer the disadvantaged.

    a. You're selfish, cold, and fearful.

    b. You're warm, understanding, and patient.

    c. You prefer the rich, but you'll help the poor if asked.

11. I'm going in for a meeting with the "big boss."

    a. I haven't an appointment for the meeting.

    b. I don't need to attend the meeting.

    c. I'll be present for the meeting.

12. We pounded the pavement for an apartment until we were successful.

    a. We found an apartment by reading the For Rent section of the newspaper.

    b. We found an apartment with new driveway pavement.

    c. We walked on every street until we found an apartment.

Exercise 14

Supply the appropriate preposition in each sentence. Use *by, to, at, on, in.*

1. He lives ＿＿＿＿＿＿ Maple Street.

2. She lives ＿＿＿＿＿＿ 440 Tarpin Avenue.

3. The plane will arrive ＿＿＿＿＿＿ International Airport this evening.

4. We arrived ＿＿＿＿＿＿ Boston last night.

5. They came ＿＿＿＿＿＿ 9:00 p.m.

6. He arrived _____ car.

7. The building is _____ Highland Street.

8. We are going _____ school.

9. I live _____ that house.

10. The bus is going to arrive _____ this corner shortly.

11. She parked her car _____ the driveway.

12. _____ first, we didn't understand anything he said.

13. Be here _____ noon!

14. We went _____ bus to New York City.

15. They live _____ Hudson, New Hampshire.

Lesson 4

Giving It Your Best Shot

David: Ana, I'm leaving! ***I'm off*** to my job interview at Dynamic Corporation.

Ana: You look great, David! You don't feel uptight, do you?

David: No, not really. I ***plan on*** going in there and ***giving it my best shot.***

Ana: Well, you certainly spent a lot of time ***filling out*** your job application.

David: I know I did. I needed ***to come directly to the point.***

Ana: I think they'll realize that you ***catch on*** quickly and will make it as a leader.

David: Well, by being totally ***up front,*** they'll know exactly what I want.

Ana: They'll be impressed with you, David, I'm sure. You've ***picked up*** good English, you've learned essential English words ***by heart,*** you know your work ***inside out.*** What more could they ask for?

David: And I like people, too. That's important.

Ana: Most definitely. David, you'll have it made. You're a real *go-getter.*

David: That, we both are! And we do plan *to get ahead* in life!

Definitions

to be off: to leave, to go
Where are you off to now? Where are you going now?

to plan on: to intend to, to have plans to, to want to
She plans on having a salad for lunch. She wants to have a salad for lunch.

to give it one's best shot: to try one's best, to do the best one can do
When I went to the interview, I gave it my best shot. I did the best I could do in presenting myself.

to fill out: to complete with information, to write information
Please fill out the application. Write your personal information such as name, address, and profession.

to come to the point: to say exactly what one intends to say, to be direct in speech or writing
Come to the point. Tell me clearly and directly what you want to know.

to catch on: to learn, to comprehend, to understand
The new employee catches on quickly. She learns fast.

up front: honest, sincere, open
She was up front about her professional abilities. She was honest about her abilities.

to pick up: to learn easily, to gain knowledge without really trying
Children can pick up a language without really trying. Children can learn a language easily.

by heart: through memorization
Learn the instructions by heart. Memorize the instructions.

inside out: thoroughly, completely, perfectly
He knows his business inside out. He understands it thoroughly.

go-getter: a person with a strong desire to succeed, a hard worker
He's a real go-getter. He's a hard worker.

to get ahead: to succeed, to advance
I want to get ahead in life! I want to succeed in life!

The following idioms may be separated by the object. These idioms may be said two ways.

to fill out:

He is filling out the form.

He is filling the form out.

to pick up:

She picked up algebra quickly.

She picked algebra up quickly.

Exercise 1

Answer these questions from the dialogue orally.

1. Where is David off to?
2. What does he plan on doing?
3. How can he give it his best shot?
4. What did David spend a lot of time filling out?
5. Why did he need to come directly to the point?
6. What does Ana mean when she says David catches on quickly?
7. Why is it good for David to be totally up front?
8. What has David picked up and learned by heart?
9. How well does David know his work if he knows it inside out?
10. Are both David and Ana go-getters?
11. Do you think they will get ahead in life? Why?

Exercise 2

Write the idioms from the dialogue that correspond to the words in parentheses.

1. David (is going) _____ to a job interview at Dynamic Corporation.

2. He (intends) _____ doing his best.

3. He intends (to do his best) _____ .

4. David spent a lot of time (writing information on) _____

   _____ the application.

5. He needed (to be direct in saying what he wanted) _____

_____ .

6. He (learns) _____ quickly.

7. He is being totally (honest) _____ in what he
wants to do.

8. David has (learned easily) _____ good
English.

9. He's learned the essential English words (through memorization)

_____ .

10. David knows his work (perfectly) _____ .

11. Both David and Ana are (hard workers) _____ .

12. They both plan (to succeed) _____ in life.

Exercise 3
Answer these questions orally.

1. What do you plan on doing with your life?
2. When was the last time you filled out a job application?
3. Will you be off to an interview anytime soon?
4. How will you give it your best shot?
5. Do you come to the point when you're being interviewed?
6. What kind of material do you have to know by heart for your profession?
7. What kind of material do you still need to pick up?
8. How well do you know your job if you know it inside out?
9. Do you catch on quickly to new jobs?
10. Are you totally up front when you need to discuss something?
11. Do you consider yourself a go-getter who will get ahead in life?

Exercise 4
Match the idiom to its definition by writing the letter of the definition on the line next to the idiom number.

1. _____ inside out   a. to succeed

2. _____ to plan on   b. to comprehend

3. _____ to get ahead   c. to try one's best

4. _____ to come to the point   d. to intend to

5. _____ go-getter   e. to write information

6. _____ to catch on   f. through memorization

7. _____ up front   g. to learn easily

8. _____ to pick up   h. perfectly

9. _____ by heart   i. hard worker

10. _____ to fill out   j. to leave

11. _____ to be off   k. to be direct in speech

12. _____ to give it one's best   l. sincere
    shot

Exercise 5
Respond to these statements orally.

1. Give three items you must write when you fill out a charge card application.
2. Give one way to learn something inside out.
3. Give two ways to get ahead in life.
4. Name two things you plan on doing tomorrow.
5. Name four idioms you know by heart.
6. Name two places you are off to every day.

Exercise 6
Underline the words in parentheses that best correspond to the italicized idioms.

1. Whenever he starts something new, he *gives it his best shot.* He (meditates, tries his best, learns quickly).
2. Children *pick up* languages quickly. They (can't learn, easily learn, have difficulty learning) languages.
3. They *filled out* the form incorrectly. They (wrote information, read what they had written, memorized the material) incorrectly.
4. We know the rules and regulations *by heart.* We (are learning, are trying to remember, memorized) them.
5. He *plans on* attending all meetings. He (wants to, won't, has no plans to) attend all meetings.
6. Because she is *up front,* we know exactly what she wants. She is (insincere, open, dishonest) about her desires.
7. We *are off* to work every morning. We (leave from, leave for, don't go to) work every morning.
8. *Come to the point!* (Don't say what you mean, Say what you mean, Be indirect in your speech)!
9. Did you *catch on* to the new job? Did you (understand, complete, finish) the new job?
10. She has always been a *go-getter.* She (procrastinates, has few expectations, has a strong desire to succeed).
11. He *got ahead* in his profession. He (advanced, was unsuccessful, regressed) in his profession.
12. She knows her occupation *inside out.* She knows it (exceptionally well, moderately well, fairly well).

Exercise 7
Reread the dialogue. Tell the story in your own words using the idioms.

Exercise 8
Complete the second sentence by substituting idioms for the italicized words.

1. I am learning the idioms *through memorization.*

   I am learning the idioms _____ .

2. A *hard-working person* will be rewarded.

A _____ will be rewarded.

3. We *are going* to California.

We _____ to California.

4. What do you *intend to* do?

What do you _____ doing?

5. He is trying *to advance* in his position at the bank.

He is trying _____ in his position at the

bank.

6. When he took the exam, he *did the best he could do.*

When he took the exam, he _____ .

7. She *learned* a lot of English when she was in Nashua, New Hampshire.

She _____ a lot of English when she was in
Nashua, New Hampshire.

8. You have to *complete* this form.

You have to _____ this form.

9. People like him because he *is direct in speech.*

People like him because he _____ .

10. I know this information *thoroughly.*

I know this information _____ .

11. David *understands* fast.

David _____ fast.

12. She is *honest* with her boss.

She is _____ with her boss.

Exercise 9
Change these sentences to questions by using a question word (*when, how, who, where, what*) for the italicized words.

Example: *He* has put in many hours of study.

_____*Who*_____ has put in many hours of study?

1. They plan on attending *the dance*.

   _____ do they plan on attending?

2. She is off to *New York* for the week.

   _____ is she off to for the week?

3. *Ana* will get ahead.

   _____ will get ahead?

4. David is filling out the insurance forms *now*.

   _____ is David filling out the insurance forms?

5. She is *up front* with most people.

   _____ is she with most people?

6. *I* am a go-getter.

   _____ is a go-getter?

7. She learned the numbers by heart *yesterday*.

   _____ did she learn the numbers by heart?

8. They tried *to give it their best shot*.

   _____ did they try to do?

9. He *came to the point* immediately.

   _____ did he do immediately?

10. She caught on to the terminology *very quickly.*

_____ did she catch on to the terminology?

11. We picked up the *information* very quickly.

_____ did we pick up very quickly?

12. They know their business *inside out.*

_____ do they know their business?

Exercise 10
Complete the idiom phrase in each sentence.

1. If you want to get _____ , you have to work hard.

2. They learned everything so well, they knew it all _____ heart.

3. We are _____ to a party; do you want to come?

4. I plan _____ being there by 8:00 p.m.

5. If you know something thoroughly, you know it _____ out.

6. He's a very hard worker. Everyone knows he's a go- _____ .

7. Are you good at picking _____ languages?

8. Usually, new employees _____ on quickly to this job. It isn't very difficult.

9. Even though he gave it his _____ _____ , he still didn't make it.

10. If you say exactly what you mean, you come to the _____ .

11. Everyone likes her because she's always up _____ and truthful.

12. How long did it take you to fill _____ the application?

Exercise 11
With a partner, create and perform an interesting, funny, enjoyable dialogue. Use as many idioms from this lesson as possible.

Exercise 12
Write sentences with the idioms given.

1. to pick up (write the sentence in two ways)

_____

_____

2. to be off

_____

3. to plan on

_____

4. by heart

_____

5. to get ahead

_____

6. to fill out (write the sentence in two ways)

_____

_____

7. up front

_____

8. to catch on

_____

Exercise 13

Circle the letter of the sentence that corresponds to the idiom used in the numbered sentence.

1. He caught on quickly to the American way of life.

   a. He doesn't really understand the American way of life.

   b. He understands the American way of life.

   c. He has no knowledge of the American way of life.

2. They are very up front in their relationship with each other.

   a. They tell each other exactly what they feel.

   b. They don't come to the point.

   c. They have difficulty being honest.

3. She tried to get ahead socially. ·

   a. She didn't like people.

   b. She wanted to be popular.

   c. She was antisocial.

4. They filled the income tax forms out last month.

   a. They completed them.

   b. They memorized them.

   c. They failed to write the information.

5. David picked up auto mechanics from watching his friend.

   a. He learned about auto mechanics from watching his friend.

   b. He studied hard.

   c. He tried very hard to learn about auto mechanics.

6. The child knows the poem by heart.

   a. He memorized the poem.

   b. He read the poem.

   c. He forgot the poem.

7. I'm off to the theater again.

   a. I'm leaving the theater.

   b. I'm still at the theater.

   c. I'm going to the theater.

8. The woman plans on fulfilling her lifelong wish.

   a. She had abandoned her wish.

   b. She dreams about what she wants to do.

   c. She intends to complete what she wants to do.

9. When he entered the cooking contest, he gave it his best shot.

   a. He didn't try very hard, but he won the contest.

   b. He decided not to enter the contest.

   c. He made the best meal he could.

10. He came directly to the point and told him to leave.

    a. He was indirect in telling him to leave.

    b. He specifically told him to leave.

    c. He didn't tell him to leave.

11. She knows her husband inside out.

    a. She hardly understands him.

    b. She understands him fairly well.

    c. She understands him exceptionally well.

12. He's been a go-getter ever since his family can remember.

    a. He has no expectations.

    b. He always procrastinates.

    c. He's very ambitious.

Exercise 14

Supply the appropriate preposition in each sentence. Use *out, in, off, to, on, of, up*.

1. He found _____ everything he needs to know to decide.

2. We can count _____ him to be here at noon; he's always punctual.

3. In spite _____ their differences, they decided to marry sooner.

4. I've set my sights _____ a house near the ocean.

5. What do you have _____ do?

6. Drop this _____ at the laundry, please.

7. We saw tons _____ flowers at the flower festival.

8. I'm not mixed _____ ! I know what I'm doing!

9. What do you mean, you can't keep _____ ? Try harder!

10. You can sign _____ here for a free prize.

11. Did you fill _____ the sweepstakes form?

12. I'll stop _____ to see you later this morning.

13. Where do you plan _____ going for your honeymoon?

14. Do you think you can make _____ well in that kind of business?

15. Where is he _____ to now? He's never at home!

Lesson 5

Behind the Wheel

David: Well, Ana, today's the day you're **going for** your driver's license. Do you think you're ready for the test?

Ana: I certainly hope so! I've **put in** so many hours of **behind the wheel** training, and I've **gone through** the driving manual so many times, I should be perfect!

David: Well, you've certainly done lots of **starting up** on hills and **backing up** into parking places.

Ana: As well as **looking out for** other drivers and maneuvering around potholes!

David: How do you feel about the **road signs**? Have you mastered all their shapes and meanings?

Ana: I certainly have. Actually, I feel as though I've **taken advantage of** every learning experience available. Yet, I still feel uptight about the **road test**.

David: Don't worry, Ana. Just **take your time.** With your determination and know-how, you'll pass the test **with flying colors**!

Definitions

to go for: to try to get or acquire, to intend to obtain
When will Ana go for her license? When will she try to get it?

to put in: to spend time doing something, to utilize time
She put in three hours of study. She spent three hours studying.

behind the wheel: driving a vehicle
He's behind the wheel! He's driving!

to go through: to study, to read, to examine
He went through all the materials. He read them carefully.

to start up: to begin operating or performing
He started up the car and left. He began operating the car and left.

to back up: to drive backwards, to go in a reverse direction
He backed up carefully into the parking area. He drove backwards carefully.

to look out for: to watch for, to be watchful of, to be careful of
Look out for that car! Be careful of that car!

road sign: a signal that alerts drivers to a road or traffic situation
The road sign showed a sharp right turn. The sign on the road indicated a sharp turn to the right.

to take advantage of: to use an opportunity to one's benefit, to benefit from
Take advantage of free education. Benefit from the opportunity of free education.

road test: a test to examine one's driving ability
The road test was easy. The test that examined his driving ability was not difficult.

with flying colors: with exceptional success, exceptionally well
She passed the test with flying colors. She did exceptionally well on the test.

to take one's time: to move slowly, to be unhurried, not to rush
Take your time! Don't rush!

The following idioms may be separated by the object. These idioms may be said in two ways.

to put in:
   He has put in many hours.
   He has put many hours in.

to start up:
   Can you start up the car?
   Can you start the car up?

to back up:
   Back up the truck.
   Back the truck up.

Exercise 1
Answer these questions from the dialogue orally.

1. When is Ana going for her driver's license?
2. How many hours of behind the wheel training has she put in?
3. How well has she gone through the driving manual?
4. Where has she learned to start up?
5. Can she back up into parking places?
6. Whom and what must she look out for?
7. What has she learned about the road signs?
8. What has she taken advantage of?
9. Why do you think Ana is uptight about the road test?
10. Does David think Ana will pass the test if she takes her time? Why?
11. How will she pass the test if she passes it with flying colors?

Exercise 2
Write the idioms from the dialogue that correspond to the words in parentheses.

1. Ana is (trying to acquire) _____ her driver's license.

2. She has (spent) _____ many hours of driving.

3. She has spent hours (driving a vehicle) _____

   _____ .

4. Ana has (studied) _____ the manual
   carefully.

5. She has practiced (beginning to operate the car) _____
   on hills.

6. She has practiced (driving backwards) _____
   into parking places.

7. Ana has learned (to watch for) _____ other
   drivers.

8. She has mastered the (signals that alert drivers to road and traffic

   situations) _____ .

9. Ana has (benefited from) _____ every
   learning experience available.

10. She is uptight about the (test that examines her driving ability)

    _____ .

11. Ana must (not hurry) _____ .

12. David is certain Ana will pass the test (exceptionally well) _____

    _____ .

Exercise 3
Answer these questions orally.

1. When did you, or will you, go for your driver's license?
2. Were you, or will you be, uptight about the road test?
3. Do you take your time on tests?
4. Do you usually pass tests with flying colors?
5. Have you gone through the driving manual carefully?
6. How many hours of driver's training have you put in?

7. How do you do behind the wheel?

8. What kind of parking places have you learned to back up into?

9. Can you start up easily on a hill?

10. Why must you look out for other drivers?

11. What information do road signs give?

12. What kind of driving situations have you taken advantage of?

Exercise 4

Match the idiom to its definition by writing the letter of the definition on the line next to the idiom number.

1. _____ road test

2. _____ to go for

3. _____ to take advantage of

4. _____ road sign

5. _____ to look out for

6. _____ to take one's time

7. _____ to put in

8. _____ to start up

9. _____ with flying colors

10. _____ to back up

11. _____ behind the wheel

12. _____ to go through

a. to be watchful

b. to go in a reverse direction

c. to benefit from an opportunity

d. a test to examine one's driving ability

e. exceptionally well

f. to try to acquire

g. driving a vehicle

h. to study

i. not to rush

j. to spend time

k. to begin operating

l. a signal that alerts drivers to a road or traffic situation

Exercise 5
Respond to these statements orally.

1. Name two places you can back up into.
2. Name two hazards you must look out for while driving.
3. Name one way to pass a test with flying colors.
4. Give two reasons for doing behind the wheel training.
5. Give three conditions indicated by road signs.
6. Give one reason for going for a driver's license.

Exercise 6
Underline the words in parentheses that best correspond to the italicized idioms.

1. She *takes her time* when she drives. She (hurries, doesn't hurry, rushes).
2. He *backed up* and hit the garage. He drove (carefully, in a reverse direction, in a forward direction).
3. There were various *road signs* before the dangerous intersection. There were (workers, signals, pedestrians).
4. How much time did you *put in* memorizing the rules? How much time did you (spend, think about, worry about) memorizing the rules?
5. He took the *road test*. He (demonstrated his writing ability, demonstrated his driving ability, failed to drive a vehicle).
6. He was *behind the wheel* when it happened. He was (a passenger, sitting in the back seat, driving).
7. She will *go for* her license next week. She will (examine, study, try to obtain) her license next week.
8. You must *look out for* the potholes. You must (back into, enter, be careful of) the potholes.
9. She passed the writing test *with flying colors*. She did (fairly well, exceptionally well, quite well).
10. He *took advantage of* the free driving classes. He (was unable to attend, attended, couldn't attend) the free driving classes.
11. He *went through* the manual several times. He (glanced at, studied, ignored) the manual.
12. What happened when you *started up* the car? What happened when you (stopped the engine, began operating the motor, stepped on the brake)?

Exercise 7
Reread the dialogue. Tell the story in your own words using the idioms.

Exercise 8
Complete the second sentence by substituting idioms for the italicized words.

1. He's finally *driving a vehicle*!

   He's finally _____ !

2. It's difficult *to begin operating the car* on a hill.

   It's difficult _____ on a hill.

3. You must *drive backwards* carefully.

   You must _____ carefully.

4. The *test to examine his driving ability* was this morning.

   The _____ was this morning.

5. She *did not rush* during the test.

   She _____ during the test.

6. She *spent* many hours learning the driving rules.

   She _____ many hours learning the driving rules.

7. She hopes to pass the examination *extremely well*.

   She hopes to pass the examination _____ .

8. He will *try to obtain* his license tomorrow.

   He will _____ his license tomorrow.

9. If you *study* the manual carefully, you will do well.

   If you _____ the manual carefully, you will do well.

10. *Benefit from* driving in the quiet hours of the evening.

   _____ driving in the quiet hours of the evening.

11. The *signals that alert drivers to road situations* are of various sizes.

   The _____ are of various sizes.

12. *Be careful of* the pedestrians!

   _____ the pedestrians!

Exercise 9
Change these sentences to the future form. Use *going to*.

Example: She *is taking* notes.

   She *is going to take* notes.

1. The road test *is* easy.

   The road test _____ easy.

2. He *went* through the book carefully.

   He _____ through the book carefully.

3. She *took* advantage of the low gasoline prices.

   She _____ advantage of the low gasoline prices.

4. They *learn* the road signs easily.

   They _____ the road signs easily.

5. He *likes* to be behind the wheel.

   He _____ to be behind the wheel.

6. *Did* she *go* for a driver's license application?

   _____ she _____ for a driver's license application?

7. He *backed* up into the bus.

   He _____ up into the bus.

8. They *will try* to pass the test with flying colors.

   They _____ to pass the test with flying colors.

9. He *started* the tractor up very easily.

   He _____ the tractor up very easily.

10. How much time *will* they *put* in?

    How much time _____ they _____ in?

11. We *will look* out for pedestrians.

    We _____ out for pedestrians.

12. Why *do* they *take* their time?

    Why _____ they _____ their time?

Exercise 10
Complete the idiom phrase in each sentence.

1. Let's take _____ of the shortcut to work. We need to get there quickly.

2. She did so well that she finished the driving test with _____ colors.

3. Look _____ _____ the children crossing the road. Don't hit them!

4. When you start _____ on a hill, put your foot on the brake.

5. He backed _____ so fast that he hit the fence.

6. She loves driving now that she is old enough to be behind the

   _____ .

7. _____ your time. Drive slowly and carefully.

8. He drove down Main Street as part of the _____ test for his driving license.

9. If we follow the road _____ , we will know exactly which roads to take.

10. When did you go _____ your license?

11. He put _____ thirty hours of driving before taking the test.

12. How many times did you have to go _____ the manual to learn it by heart?

Exercise 11
With a partner, create and perform an interesting, funny, enjoyable dialogue. Use as many idioms from this lesson as possible.

Exercise 12
Write sentences with the idioms given.

1. to look out for

   _____

2. to go for

   _____

3. to put in (write the sentence in two ways)

   _____

   _____

4. to back up (write the sentence in two ways)

   _____

   _____

5. behind the wheel

_____

6. to take advantage of

_____

7. to take one's time

_____

8. with flying colors

_____

Exercise 13
Circle the letter of the sentence that corresponds to the idiom used in the numbered sentence.

1. Take your time when you eat.
   a. Watch the clock when you eat.
   b. Hurry when you eat.
   c. Don't hurry when you eat.
2. They took advantage of the low interest mortgage rate.
   a. They decided against taking the low interest mortgage rate.
   b. They weren't certain they could afford the low interest mortgage payments.
   c. They decided to take the low interest mortgage rate.
3. The machine started up immediately.
   a. It stalled.
   b. It began operating.
   c. It didn't operate.
4. The workmen placed road signs at their work site.
   a. Drivers were informed of a rest area.
   b. Drivers were advised to drive fast.
   c. Drivers were advised to drive carefully.
5. He passed the swimming test with flying colors.
   a. He had mediocre results in the swimming test.
   b. He did extremely well in the swimming test.
   c. He was fairly successful in the swimming test.

6. She had to back the bus up to leave the parking area.

    a. She had to go in a reverse direction.

    b. She had to go in a forward direction.

    c. She couldn't leave the parking area.

7. She's going for first prize in the cooking contest.

    a. She's not trying to get first prize.

    b. She doesn't want first prize.

    c. She wants first prize.

8. The children were given a road test for bicycle riding.

    a. The safety of their bicycles was tested.

    b. Their ability to ride a bicycle was tested.

    c. Their ability to repair a bicycle was tested.

9. They went through the inventory before purchasing supplies.

    a. They examined the inventory.

    b. They were uptight about the inventory.

    c. They ignored the inventory.

10. The children were told to look out for glass in the play area.

    a. They were told to be careless.

    b. They were told to be careful.

    c. They were told to be unobservant.

11. He was behind the wheel at the racetrack.

    a. He was driving at the racetrack.

    b. He was repairing wheels at the racetrack.

    c. He was the announcer at the racetrack.

12. She put four years in as an airplane pilot.

    a. She flew an airplane four times.

    b. As a pilot, she flew four airplanes.

    c. She was an airplane pilot for four years.

Exercise 14
Supply the appropriate preposition in each sentence for the word *look*.
Use the dictionary as needed. Choose from the following expressions:

to look out	to look over
to look out (through)	to look after
to look up	to look in the eye
to look down on	to look in on
to look for	to look at

1. What does this word mean?

   I don't know. Look it _____ in the dictionary.

2. Look _____ that picture. Isn't it beautiful?

3. Look me _____ the eye. It will be more evident if you are lying or not.

4. Look _____ the window at the beautiful foliage!

5. Look _____ my homework, please. I don't know if it's correct or not.

6. Look _____ the children for the evening. Take good care of them.

7. I lost my key, and I don't know where to look _____ it.

8. Look _____ ! Don't fall into that big hole in the ground!

9. He thinks he's so wonderful; nobody really likes him.

   You're right. He always looks _____ _____ everyone.

10. Look _____ _____ Lizzy, Joe. I heard she broke her toe; but don't stay too long.

Review of Lessons 1–5

Exercise 1
Write the correct form of the best idiom for each italicized definition.
Use each idiom once.

to pick up	to burn the midnight oil
to have what it takes	by air
to give it one's best shot	to be off
with flying colors	to plan on
little by little	to make out
up front	road test
to go through	to take one's time
tired out	to have a chance
to have to	to take notes
to go in for	to keep up

1. The examiner gave him a *test to determine his driving ability.*

   The examiner gave him a _____ .

2. The men were *exhausted* after repairing the driveway.

   The men were _____ after repairing the
   driveway.

3. They *did* well on their business venture.

   They _____ well on their business venture.

4. If she *doesn't rush,* she will do a good job.

   If she _____ , she will do a good job.

5. The students *wrote information* on the teacher's lecture.

   The students _____ on the teacher's lecture.

6. She *intends to* be a dentist.

   She _____ being a dentist.

7. A doctor *must* study for many years to learn the profession.

   A doctor _____ study for many years to learn the profession.

8. He *learned* English in a month.

   He _____ English in a month.

9. She is *studying* the manual carefully.

   She is _____ the manual carefully.

10. They *have the possibility* of finding the stolen diamonds.

    They _____ of finding the stolen diamonds.

11. They *have the abilities* to start an antique business.

    They _____ to start an antique business.

12. They arrived *in an airplane*.

    They arrived _____ .

13. They won the race *exceptionally well*.

    They won the race _____ .

14. He will be completely *open* in his speech.

    He will be completely _____ in his speech.

15. At the university, they *study late into the night*.

    At the university, they _____ .

16. Even though he was *doing the best he could do,* his family still wasn't satisfied.

    Even though he was _____ , his family still wasn't satisfied.

17. You could *maintain the same pace as* the others if you would get more sleep.

    You could _____ with the others if you would get more sleep.

18. He *went* to the battle zone during the war.

    He _____ to the battle zone during the war.

19. *Gradually*, the handicapped child learned to walk.

    _____ , the handicapped child learned to walk.

20. She *has an appointment for* her evaluation this afternoon.

    She's _____ her evaluation this afternoon.

Exercise 2
Choose the idiom in parentheses that best completes the sentence.

1. He must learn how to _____ an application before applying for a job. (keep up, fill out, pick up)

2. They _____ until they found an apartment. (looked out for, got ahead, pounded the pavement)

3. He _____ after years of hard work. (started up, made it, signed up)

4. People can _____ any situation if necessary. (go in for, get used to, move ahead)

5. When the new driver _____ , he crashed into the garage. (caught on, got ahead, backed up)

6. She _____ marrying a wealthy man who could give her the things she wanted. (set her sights on, kept up, put in)

7. In spite of not knowing _____ , he is a very optimistic person. (road signs, up front, which way to turn)

8. For a man with no education, he _____ .
   (has a lot to offer, picked up, signed up)

9. When she _____ , everyone was impressed.
   (stopped in, dropped off, was off)

10. They _____ so many problems in their
    lives that they can handle anything. (got through, set their sights on,
    kept up)

11. She _____ ! She has personality, intelligence,
    beauty, and wealth! (has to offer, has it made, pays attention)

12. A person who is _____ is confused. (go-
    getter, up front, mixed up)

13. We have to _____ if we plan to be there this
    evening. (get going, get ahead, keep up)

14. They will _____ their friends at the theatre.
    (look out for, drop off, check out)

15. Once he decided _____ with his plans,
    nothing could stop him. (to keep up, to count on, to move ahead)

16. I know this material _____ , and I can pass
    the test easily. (in spite of, with flying colors, inside out)

17. She _____ forty hours of training before
    applying for the license. (put in, caught on, dropped off)

18. The children in that class are _____ winning
    the competition. (counting on, moving ahead, checking out)

19. Once she decided to be a lawyer, she went to college and _____

    _____ . (came to the point, kept up, gave it all she's got)

20. When the boys _____ that they had taken
    the wrong bus, they told the bus driver. (got going, looked out for,
    found out)

Exercise 3
Write the best idiom for each sentence. Use each idiom once.

broken English   comes to the point
took advantage of   take my word
signed up   pay attention
in spite of   by heart
started up   behind the wheel
going for   check out
at first   at the same time
catch on   road signs
got ahead   tons of
look out for   go-getter

1. The students _____ for five courses at the university yesterday.

2. _____ , if you think positively, everything will be all right.

3. The reckless driver failed to follow the _____ that indicated road conditions.

4. They're _____ their marriage license at city hall.

5. _____ he was uptight about meeting his girlfriend's parents.

6. Because she is fast to grasp new situations, she will _____

   _____ to the job quickly.

7. We know exactly what he means because he _____

   _____ immediately.

8. _____ financial problems, they still live well.

9. If you _____ to the teacher, you will understand the directions.

10. The pedestrian was hit by a car because he didn't _____

   _____ traffic as he was crossing the street.

11. She learned every spelling word _____ and
   now is ready for the spelling test.

12. The teenagers study and listen to the radio _____

   _____ .

13. There were _____ applicants for that one
   modeling position.

14. Since he's a reckless driver, no one will ride with him when he's

   _____ .

15. The wealthy entrepreneurs _____ through
   hard work and determination.

16. Even though she's been in the United States for many years, she still

   speaks _____ .

17. They _____ the free
   transportation and used it daily.

18. He _____ the car and began to drive.

19. _____ every detail of the contract before you
   sign it.

20. Ana is a _____ who will succeed in whatever
   she does.

Lesson 6

As Hungry as a Horse

Ana: Let's **go out** to lunch, David. I'd really like **to eat out** and relax.

David: I agree, Ana. We need **to take a break. How about** Express Pizza?

Ana: Oh, that's a good idea! Their food is really **top-notch,** and Zak always **bends over backwards** to please his customers.

David: Should we **call in** our order or wait 'til we get there?

Ana: Let's wait 'til we get there. The service is superb, and they'll **wait on** us quickly. Anyway, I really want **to look over** the new menu.

David: I've heard they've got some great new specials we can try.

Ana: Mmmm, they do. Like veggie supreme calzones, spinach pizza special, baklava that's **out of this world,** seafood à la . . .

David: Ana, Ana, that's enough! Let's get going, please! It **sounds like** you're **as hungry as a horse**!

Definitions

to go out: to go somewhere for enjoyment, to attend social functions
David and Ana are going out tonight. They are going dancing.

to eat out: to eat in a restaurant, to go out to eat

Let's eat out tonight. Let's eat in a restaurant.

to take a break: to stop or rest for a short time, to be free

Take a break from work. Stop for a short while and relax.

how about: what is your opinion of, what do you think of

How about going at 5:00? What do you think of going at 5:00?

top-notch: the best quality, superb, fantastic, extraordinary

This is a top-notch restaurant. This is one of the best restaurants.

to bend over backwards: to try very hard, to put much effort into

He bends over backwards to please us. He tries very hard to please us.

to call in: to inform or order by telephone

We called in our order to the pizza shop. We told them by phone what we wanted to eat.

to wait on: to serve someone, to perform services for someone

The waitress waits on her customers. She serves them their food.

to look over: to read, to examine, to peruse

They are looking over the menu. They are reading it.

out of this world: exceptionally good, extraordinary, fantastic, the best quality

The food is out of this world! It is exceptionally delicious.

to sound like (to seem like): to appear, to seem

It sounds like you're very tired. It seems as if you're very tired.

as hungry as a horse: very hungry, famished

Ana's as hungry as a horse! She is very hungry.

The following idioms may be separated by the object. These idioms may be said in two ways:

to call in:

We called in our food order.

We called our food order in.

to look over:

Let's look over the menu.

Let's look the menu over.

Exercise 1
Answer these questions from the dialogue orally.

1. Why does Ana want to go out to lunch?
2. Does David feel they need to take a break and eat out?
3. What is Ana's reaction when David says, "How about Express Pizza?"
4. What does Ana mean by top-notch food and baklava that's out of this world?
5. How might Zak bend over backwards to please his customers?
6. Do David and Ana call in their order? Why?
7. How do they wait on their customers at Express Pizza?
8. Why does Ana want to look over the new menu?
9. What does David mean when he says Ana sounds like she's as hungry as a horse?

Exercise 2
Write the idioms from the dialogue that correspond to the words in parentheses.

1. David and Ana enjoy (going somewhere) _____ to lunch.

2. They like (to eat in a restaurant) _____ and relax.

3. They need (to stop for a short while) _____ .

4. David asks Ana, "(What do you think of) _____ Express Pizza?"

5. The food at Express Pizza is (superb) _____

   _____ .

6. Zak (tries very hard) _____ to please the customers.

7. David and Ana decide not (to order by phone) _____

   _____ their order.

8. They (serve) _____ customers quickly at
   Express Pizza.

9. Ana wants (to read) _____ the menu.

10. The baklava is (exceptionally good) _____

    _____ .

11. It (seems) _____ Ana is very hungry.

12. It seems Ana is (very hungry) _____ .

Exercise 3
Answer these questions orally.

1. How often do you go out to lunch?
2. Do you enjoy eating out?
3. Do you often call in an order, or do you need to look over a menu?
4. What does it mean when you say to a friend, "I'm going out to dinner, how about you?"
5. Where might you find a restaurant that's out of this world?
6. Do you know any restaurants where they bend over backwards to wait on their customers?
7. What do you consider top-notch food?
8. If someone is as hungry as a horse, what does that sound like to you?
9. What do you do when you take a break from work?

Exercise 4
Match the idiom to its definition by writing the letter of the definition
on the line next to the idiom number.

1. _____ to bend over backwards   a. fantastic

2. _____ to eat out   b. to serve someone

3. _____ to call in   c. to seem

4. _____ to wait on   d. very hungry

5. _____ out of this world   e. to put much effort into

6. _____ how about   f. to eat in a restaurant

7. _____ to go out   g. to order by telephone

8. _____ to take a break   h. to read

9. _____ top-notch   i. what is your opinion of

10. _____ as hungry as a horse   j. to rest for a short while

11. _____ to look over   k. exceptionally good

12. _____ to sound like   l. to attend social functions

Exercise 5
Respond to these statements orally.

1. Name one restaurant where the service is out of this world.
2. Name two places where you like to eat out during the week.
3. Name one place to buy top-notch food.
4. Name one restaurant where you can call in an order.
5. Give one reason why you like, or don't like, to be waited on.
6. Name two places to go out to on the weekend.
7. Name one person who bends over backwards for you.
8. Give one time during the day that you like to take a break.

Exercise 6
Underline the words in parentheses that best correspond to the italicized idioms.

1. They serve *top-notch* oriental food. They serve (excellent, mediocre, fair) oriental food.
2. We *eat out* occasionally. We eat (at work, in the house, at a restaurant).
3. Sometimes I'm *as hungry as a horse*. Sometimes I'm (hungry, very hungry, a little hungry).
4. The restaurant is *out of this world*. It is (fairly good, rather good, exceptionally good).

5. It *sounds like* you're tired. It (is ridiculous, is absurd, appears) that you're tired.

6. A waitress *waits on* customers in a restaurant. She (serves, cooks for, samples the food of) her customers.

7. They *go out* often. They (sit in the yard, go to parties, stay home).

8. Let's *call in* our order. Let's order (at the restaurant, when the waitress comes, by phone).

9. I *look over* the menu before ordering my meal. I (memorize, read, return) the menu.

10. He *bends over backwards* for every order. He (tries hard, hardly tries, somewhat tries) for every order.

11. He *takes a break* in the afternoon. He (continues working, stops working, works hard) in the afternoon.

12. *How about* trying a new place to eat? (Why haven't we tried, What do you think of trying, When will we try) a new place to eat?

Exercise 7

Reread the dialogue. Tell the story in your own words using the idioms.

Exercise 8

Complete the second sentence by substituting idioms for the italicized words.

1. Did he *put much effort into* making the restaurant attractive?

   Did he _____ to make the restaurant attractive?

2. He *read* the menu before ordering.

   He _____ the menu before ordering.

3. The service is *exceptionally good*.

   The service is _____ .

4. Not all expensive restaurants are *the best*.

   Not all expensive restaurants are _____

   _____ .

5. It *appears* that many people will be coming.

   It _____ many people will be coming.

6. She *ordered by phone* for the whole company.

   She _____ for the whole company.

7. *What do you think of* stopping at the Oriental Food Palace after work?

   _____ stopping at the Oriental Food Palace after work?

8. If we *rest for a while,* we'll feel better.

   If we _____ , we'll feel better.

9. We like *to go somewhere for enjoyment* every Saturday.

   We like _____ every Saturday.

10. Are you really *famished*?

    Are you really _____ ?

11. We *eat in a restaurant* every week.

    We _____ every week.

12. The waitress who *serves* them is very nice.

    The waitress who _____ them is very nice.

Exercise 9
Change these sentences to the present tense.

Example: They *will try* to get ahead.

   They _____*try*_____ to get ahead.

1. He *went* out to lunch when he *finished* his work.

   He _____ out to lunch when he _____ his work.

81

2. The service *was* out of this world.

   The service _____ out of this world.

3. Ana *will call* in her order.

   Ana _____ in her order.

4. I *ate* out when I *was* with my friends.

   I _____ out when I _____ with my friends.

5. They *used to bend* over backwards to please their friends.

   They _____ over backwards to please their friends.

6. It *sounded* like they *were* in trouble.

   It _____ like they _____ in trouble.

7. They *should have taken* a break.

   They _____ a break.

8. It *was* difficult to purchase top-notch food in that country.

   It _____ difficult to purchase top-notch food in that

   country.

9. I *asked* him, "How about going out to dinner with us?"

   I _____ him, "How about going out to dinner with us?"

10. We *had looked* over the menu before we *ordered*.

    We _____ over the menu before we _____ .

11. How *could* you be as hungry as a horse?

    How _____ you be as hungry as a horse?

12. The waitress *will have waited* on him immediately.

    The waitress _____ on him immediately.

Exercise 10
Complete the idiom phrase in each sentence.

1. If you're as _____ as a _____ , you should eat something.

2. They ate _____ every night this week because they were too tired to cook.

3. Let's go _____ tonight. I'd like to go dancing.

4. Look _____ the list of movies before we choose one.

5. If you had called _____ the order, we wouldn't have to wait.

6. It _____ like he doesn't like to eat out because he always wants to eat at home.

7. Let's have him wait _____ us. He's such a friendly waiter.

8. We need to _____ a break! We've been working hard all day long.

9. Did you see that restaurant?! It's absolutely _____ of this

    _____ with a beautiful indoor garden and waterfall.

10. The meals are absolutely top- _____ too, wonderfully delicious and plentiful.

11. How _____ going to a movie with me tonight? I'm sure you'll enjoy it; it's one of your favorites.

12. They _____ over backwards to give you exactly what you want. Their service is superb.

Exercise 11
With a partner, create and perform an interesting, funny, enjoyable dialogue. Use as many idioms from this lesson as possible.

Exercise 12
Write sentences with the idioms given.

1. to look over (write the sentence in two ways)

   _____

   _____

2. to take a break

   _____

3. to sound like

   _____

4. to wait on

   _____

5. to eat out

   _____

6. out of this world

   _____

7. to call in (write the sentence in two ways)

   _____

   _____

8. to go out

   _____

Exercise 13
Circle the letter of the sentence that corresponds to the idiom used in the numbered sentence.

1. He bent over backwards to make her happy.

   a. He wanted to make her happy.

   b. He wanted his wife to listen to him.

   c. He hurt his back.

2. He called in sick at the company.

   a. He went to work sick.

   b. He was sick at the company.

   c. He informed them by phone that he was sick.

3. It sounded like they loved being in the United States.

   a. They planned to return to their country.

   b. They seemed to enjoy the United States.

   c. They attended evening classes in the United States.

4. Every morning they get a thirty-minute break.

   a. They work for thirty minutes.

   b. They try hard for thirty minutes.

   c. They rest for thirty minutes.

5. The party was out of this world.

   a. The party was marvelous.

   b. The party was pleasant.

   c. The party was nice.

6. We like to go out with our friends.

   a. We like to go to the movies with them.

   b. We like to invite them to our home.

   c. We like to go to work with them.

7. The tennis player played a top-notch game.

   a. The tennis player played an average game.

   b. The tennis player played a good game.

   c. The tennis player played a superior game.

8. They looked over their bills and were very upset.

   a. They examined them.

   b. They paid them promptly.

   c. They threw them in the trash.

9. The nurse waited on the patient.

   a. The nurse helped the patient.

   b. The nurse was very friendly.

   c. The nurse examined the patient's chart.

10. When they were vacationing in South America, they ate out daily.

    a. They ate in their hotel room.

    b. They ate in restaurants.

    c. They ate in the parks and picnic areas.

11. How about going to the city by train?

    a. Have you been to the city by train?

    b. Do you want to go to the city by train?

    c. Can you get to the city by train?

12. After the long hike in the woods, he was as hungry as a horse.

    a. After the hike, he ate a horse.

    b. After the hike, he rode his horse home.

    c. After the hike, he was famished.

Exercise 14

Supply the appropriate preposition in each sentence for the word *get*. Use the dictionary as needed. Choose from the following expressions:

to get off	to get out of	to get in
to get on	to get up	to get around
to get to	to get at	to get by
		to get through

1. What are you going _____ ? What exactly do you mean?

2. How will we get _____ if we don't have a vehicle to go places?

3. If you want to go somewhere, you can get _____ a bus, a plane, a train, a motorcycle, or even a horse.

4. However, you must get _____ a car or truck.

5. When you arrive at your destination, you get _____ the bus, the plane, the train, the motorcycle, or the horse.

6. However, you must get _____ _____ a car or truck.

7. I can't get _____ to them. All the telephone lines are down.

8. When do we get _____ New York City? We've been traveling a long time.

9. I can't get _____ . There's no room for me to move past.

10. Even though he'd like to stay in bed, he has to get _____ and get to work.

Lesson 7

On Its Last Legs

Ana: I think our car is **on its last legs,** David! It's really not **holding up** very well.

David: You're right, Ana. It's been **acting up** all winter. I experienced difficulty in starting up the car on cold mornings and backing up on hills. There's really not very much power.

Ana: Sometimes when I'm behind the wheel, I wonder if I'll make it to my destination. That was terrible last week when the car **broke down** and **tied up** city traffic. I wasn't sure which way to turn!

David: Well, I talked to the mechanic who looked the car over, and he said it would cost **an arm and a leg** to repair it properly.

Ana: That means we're **up against** a difficult decision!

David: I know we are. Do we **put money into** this old car or do we **trade it in** for another?

Ana: I'm not sure. But if we do decide to trade it in, we'll have to start checking out some good used cars.

David: Well, before we can really **settle on** anything, we'll have to **go over** our financial situation.

Ana: Then let's do that now, David. I'm sure we can **work it out** satisfactorily.

Definitions

on one's last legs: barely operating or functioning, almost useless
  The vehicle was on its last legs. It barely operated.

to hold up: to last, to continue to function, to remain in operation
  The engine is holding up fairly well. It continues to operate.

to act up: to suddenly or unexpectedly operate improperly, not to operate properly
  Why has the carburetor been acting up? Why hasn't it been operating properly?

to break down: to stop functioning, to become useless, to fail mechanically
  The truck broke down on the highway. It stopped operating.

to tie up: to stop, to obstruct, to interfere with the passage or movement of
  When the car broke down, it tied up traffic. It stopped the other cars from moving.

an arm and a leg: a higher price than necessary, too much money, a lot of money
  He charged you an arm and a leg for the tires! He charged you too much money!

up against: threatened with, confronted with, having difficulties
  They are up against some major decisions. They are confronted with some major decisions.

to put money into: to spend money on, to invest money in
  How much money did he put into that old car? How much money did he spend on its repairs?

to trade in: to exchange an old item for a new or newer item with additional payment
  Let's trade this motorcycle in. Let's exchange it for a newer one.

to settle on: to decide on, to decide
  Which vehicle did you settle on? Which one did you decide to get?

to go over: to review, to analyze, to inspect, to examine
  He goes over his car every six months. He inspects its mechanical parts.

to work out: to solve, to find a solution to, to find a way to

They worked out the problem of financing a car. They found a way to finance it.

The following idioms may be separated by the object. These idioms may be said in two ways.

to tie up:

The accident tied up traffic.

The accident tied traffic up.

to trade in:

He will trade in his car.

He will trade his car in.

to work out:

They work out their problems.

They work their problems out.

Exercise 1

Answer these questions from the dialogue orally.

1. In what ways is David and Ana's car on its last legs and not holding up very well?
2. How has it been acting up?
3. When and where did the car break down and tie up city traffic?
4. Why did the mechanic say it would cost an arm and a leg to repair the car?
5. What kind of difficult decision are David and Ana up against?
6. How will they decide if they should put money into the car?
7. What must they go over before they can really settle on anything?
8. How do you think they will work out their car problem?

Exercise 2
Write the idioms from the dialogue that correspond to the words in parentheses.

1. David and Ana's car is (almost useless) _____

   _____ .

2. It isn't (operating) _____ very well.

3. It (operates improperly) _____ sometimes.

4. Last week the car (failed mechanically) _____ in city traffic.

5. It (obstructed) _____ city traffic.

6. The mechanic said it would cost (a lot of money) _____

   _____ to repair it.

7. David and Ana are (confronted with) _____ a difficult decision.

8. Should they (invest money in) _____ this car?

9. Should they (exchange) _____ the car?

10. Before they can (decide on) _____ anything, they have to discuss their finances.

11. They have to (analyze) _____ their financial situation.

12. Ana is sure they can (solve) _____ the problem.

Exercise 3
Answer these questions orally.

1. How is your car holding up?
2. What could be wrong with a car that's on its last legs?

3. Does your car ever act up?

4. What parts of your car cost an arm and a leg?

5. What would you do if your car broke down and tied up traffic on a busy street?

6. Would you be up against a difficult decision if your car broke down? Why?

7. Would you put money into it or would you trade it in?

8. Would you have to go over your financial situation before making a decision?

9. How could you work out the finances of trading in a car?

10. Which choice would you finally settle on and why?

Exercise 4

Match the idiom to its definition by writing the letter of the definition on the line next to the idiom number.

1. _____ to go over   a. confronted with

2. _____ to work out   b. to invest money in

3. _____ to settle on   c. almost useless

4. _____ to trade in   d. to find a solution to

5. _____ an arm and a leg   e. to continue to function

6. _____ to break down   f. to suddenly operate improperly

7. _____ on one's last legs g. to exchange one item for another

8. _____ to hold up   h. to obstruct

9. _____ up against   i. to fail mechanically

10. _____ to tie up   j. a lot of money

11. _____ to act up   k. to decide

12. _____ to put money into l. to examine

93

Exercise 5
Respond to these statements orally.

1. Give one reason for trading a car in.
2. Give one way to work a problem out.
3. Give two reasons for putting money into a vehicle.
4. Give one reason for going over your finances.
5. Name three ways in which a car can act up.
6. Name some items that cost an arm and a leg.

Exercise 6
Underline the words in parentheses that best correspond to the italicized idioms.

1. The accident *tied up* traffic for two hours. It (stopped, hardly affected, encouraged the movement of) the traffic.
2. He wants to *trade in* his motorcycle for a jeep. He plans to (have two vehicles, exchange one for the other, buy a motorcycle).
3. After much debate, they *settled on* a new car. They (decided against buying, decided to buy, exchanged) a new car.
4. She *put money into* her old car. She (exchanged it, invested money in its repairs, paid too much).
5. They must *work out* the problem. They must (find a solution to, stop trying to solve, deny) the problem.
6. The truck was *on its last legs* because it was not being maintained well. The truck was (in good condition, in excellent condition, in poor condition).
7. When they needed a second car, they were *up against* a difficult decision. They (knew, had to decide, were certain) what to do.
8. The car is *holding up* in spite of its age. It (continues to function, fails to function, is almost useless).
9. The car *acted up* for two months. The car (failed to operate, stopped functioning, didn't always operate properly).
10. The jeep *broke down* in the desert. It (continued to operate, operated poorly, stopped operating).
11. He charged *an arm and a leg* to repair the transmission. He charged (too much, too little, not enough).
12. They *went over* the airplane carefully. They (hijacked, wrecked, inspected) the airplane.

Exercise 7
Reread the dialogue. Tell the story in your own words using the idioms.

Exercise 8
Complete the second sentence by substituting idioms for the italicized words.

1. The motorcycle was *almost useless.*

   The motorcycle was _____ .

2. They *decided on* purchasing a car at a later time.

   They _____ purchasing a car at a later time.

3. It will *remain in operation* if minor repairs are made.

   It will _____ if minor repairs are made.

4. If you *exchange* your vehicle after November, you'll get a better price.

   If you _____ your vehicle after November, you'll get a better price.

5. He *spent money on* it, but it failed anyway.

   He _____ it, but it failed anyway.

6. When a car begins *to operate improperly,* it usually needs repairs.

   When a car begins _____ , it usually needs repairs.

7. She *examined* it carefully and found nothing wrong with it.

   She _____ it carefully and found nothing wrong with it.

8. Some people *find solutions to* their problems easily.

   Some people _____ their problems easily.

9. A vehicle that *stops operating* is not very useful.

   A vehicle that _____ is not very useful.

10. Although he was *confronted with* financial obligations, he was optimistic.

    Although he was _____ financial obligations, he was optimistic.

11. Items that cost *too much money* are often not worth buying.

    Items that cost _____ are often not worth buying.

12. Construction on the road *stopped* traffic in both directions.

    Construction on the road _____ traffic in both directions.

Exercise 9
Change these sentences to the future negative form. Use *won't*.

Example: He *found* out about it.

He _____*won't find*_____ out about it.

1. The car *broke* down suddenly in heavy traffic.

   The car _____ down suddenly in heavy traffic.

2. They *settled* on purchasing a van.

   They _____ on purchasing a van.

3. He *traded* in his car.

   He _____ in his car.

4. The mechanical parts *will hold* up well.

   The mechanical parts _____ up well.

5. Why *was* it on its last legs?

   Why _____ it _____ on its last legs?

6. The carburetor *acted* up again.

   The carburetor _____ up again.

7. Why *didn't* he *put* his money into a new car?

   Why _____ he _____ his money into a new car?

8. They *will work* it out successfully.

   They _____ it out successfully.

9. The mechanic *went* over the minor parts of the bus.

   The mechanic _____ over the minor parts of
   the bus.

10. It certainly *costs* an arm and a leg!

    It certainly _____ an arm and a leg!

11. The road conditions *tied* up traffic.

    The road conditions _____ up traffic.

12. They *were* up against a major car repair.

    They _____ up against a major car repair.

Exercise 10
Complete the idiom phrase in each sentence.

1. When he lost his job, he was _____ against a definite money
   problem.

2. If the refrigerator acts _____ again, we'll have to get a new
   one.

3. Let's get a new car. I want to trade _____ this one.

4. Doctors, lawyers, mechanics—they all charge an _____ and a

   _____ for their services.

5. If this fence holds _____ against the next storm, it will be a miracle!

6. When the bus broke _____ , all the children had to leave it and wait for another one.

7. We settled _____ moving to the Midwest where we have friends.

8. Go _____ the contract again. It's easy to miss an important detail.

9. The accident tied _____ traffic from here to Elm Street for two hours.

10. We can work it _____ by ourselves. We don't need anyone's help.

11. How much money do you have to put _____ this car? Whatever it is, it's too much!

12. This car has been on its last _____ for so long, maybe it'll never break down!

Exercise 11

With a partner, create and perform an interesting, funny, enjoyable dialogue. Use as many idioms from this lesson as possible.

Exercise 12
Write sentences with the idioms given.

1. to trade in (write the sentence in two ways)

_____

_____

2. to put money into

_____

3. to hold up

_____

4. to tie up (write the sentence in two ways)

_____

_____

5. to break down

_____

6. an arm and a leg

_____

7. to go over

_____

8. to settle on

_____

Exercise 13
Circle the letter of the sentence that corresponds to the idiom used in the numbered sentence.

1. We settled on pizza for lunch.
   a. We decided to eat pizza.
   b. We decided not to eat pizza.
   c. We couldn't decide what to eat.
2. The washing machine broke down again.
   a. It continues to operate.
   b. It works well.
   c. It doesn't work.
3. They worked out the mathematical problems before class.
   a. They were unable to solve the problems.
   b. They found the answers.
   c. They stopped trying to find the solutions.

4. The old man was on his last legs.

   a. He was feeling fine.

   b. He was healthy.

   c. He was dying.

5. They put money into the stock market.

   a. They bought stocks.

   b. They sold stocks.

   c. They stopped buying and selling stocks.

6. We went over our plans before leaving for the Orient.

   a. We left for the Orient.

   b. We weren't sure if we were going to the Orient.

   c. We discussed what we wanted to do in the Orient.

7. The refrigerator acts up during the hot summer months.

   a. It stops operating completely.

   b. It operates well.

   c. It doesn't always work right.

8. The doctor bills cost him an arm and a leg.

   a. The doctor undercharged him.

   b. The doctor charged exorbitant fees.

   c. The doctor didn't charge him enough.

9. The farmers were up against a drought last summer.

   a. They were delighted with the drought.

   b. They were certain of having too much water.

   c. They were afraid of having too little water.

10. The heavy ice tied the boats up on the river.

   a. The boats were unable to move.

   b. The boats made rapid progress.

   c. The boats continued moving.

11. They traded their lawn mower in for a better one.

   a. They now have two lawn mowers.

   b. They exchanged the better lawn mower.

   c. They exchanged the older lawn mower.

12. This couch will hold up for another five years.

   a. This couch won't last five more years.

   b. This couch will be good for five more years.

   c. This couch is in terrible condition.

Exercise 14
The following verbs can be followed by either the infinitive or the gerund with no change in meaning.

begin	like	start
continue	love	can't stand
hate	prefer	can't bear

Example: He can't stand *going* to school.
He can't stand *to go* to school.

1. a. He loves (ride) _____ on a motorcycle.

   b. He loves (ride) _____ on a motorcycle.

2. a. We prefer (hike) _____ in the mountains.

   b. We prefer (hike) _____ in the mountains.

3. a. It began (snow) _____ early in the morning.

   b. It began (snow) _____ early in the morning.

4. a. I can't bear (leave) _____ you.

   b. I can't bear (leave) _____ you.

5. a. They continued (drive) _____ forty miles to work each day.

   b. They continued (drive) _____ forty miles to work each day.

6. a. He absolutely hates (work) _____ !

   b. He absolutely hates (work) _____ !

7. a. She likes (be) _____ near him.

   b. She likes (be) _____ near him.

8. a. They can't stand (live) _____ in poverty.

   b. They can't stand (live) _____ in poverty.

9. a. He started (study) _____ very late.

   b. He started (study) _____ very late.

10. a. They love (be) _____ in the United States.

    b. They love (be) _____ in the United States.

Lesson 8

A Good Buy

Ana: Did you **write out** a check for the new appliances we're purchasing?

David: I'm **making it out** right now and for a lot of money, too.

Ana: Appliances certainly cost an arm and a leg, don't they?

David: They sure do. But we've **thought over** this purchase and have **talked it over at length.**

Ana: Yes, we've been waiting a long time to get new appliances. Our old ones **keep on** acting up and won't hold up much longer.

David: Well, we've taken our time finding out prices, looking over various brands, **looking into** our resources . . .

Ana: And considering the **pros and cons** of **doing without** them!

David: Well, we've discussed it inside out, Ana. I think it's wise that we **made up our minds** to go for the trade-in option. We'll be getting **a good buy,** and we know it.

Ana: That's for sure. In spite of the expense, we're definitely **getting our money's worth.**

Definitions

to write out: to complete, to write in full, to write, to make out
   Did she write out a check at the store? Did she write it at the store?

to make out: to complete, to write in full, to write out
   They made out a list of appliances. They wrote a list.

to think over: to think about, to contemplate, to consider
   We thought over his idea. We considered his idea.

to talk over: to discuss together, to talk about, to consider
   When did they talk over the purchase? When did they discuss it together?

at length: thoroughly, completely, carefully, well
   We considered the price at length. We considered it thoroughly.

to keep on: to continue, to continue repeatedly
   The refrigerator keeps on acting up. The refrigerator continues acting up.

to look into: to examine carefully, to study all aspects of, to consider
   Did they look into the offer before accepting it? Did they carefully examine the offer?

pros and cons: positive and negative points of an issue
   We discussed the pros and cons of getting a bank loan. We discussed the positive and negative points of getting a bank loan.

to do without: not to need, not to have to have, to forgo
   We can do without a new stove. We don't have to have it.

to make up one's mind: to decide, to make a decision
   How quickly he made up his mind! How quickly he decided!

a good buy: [the purchase of items] at a lower than usual price
   This car was a good buy. This car was at a lower than usual price.

to get one's money's worth: to receive the complete value of an item for the price paid
   He certainly got his money's worth! He certainly received full value for what he paid!

The following idioms may be separated by the object. These idioms may be said in two ways:

to write out:

He has written out the check.

He has written the check out.

to make out:

She is making out the list.

She is making the list out.

to think over:

We will think over the matter.

Wc will think the matter over.

to talk over:

Let's talk over the problem.

Let's talk the problem over.

Exercise 1

Answer these questions from the dialogue orally.

1. Why is David writing out a check?
2. For how much is he making it out?
3. What have David and Ana thought over and talked over at length?
4. What keeps on acting up?
5. Why have David and Ana been looking into their resources?
6. What might be the pros and cons of doing without new appliances?
7. What did Ana and David finally make up their minds to do?
8. How might they be getting a good buy?
9. What does Ana mean when she says, "We're definitely getting our money's worth"?

Exercise 2

Write the idioms from the dialogue that correspond to the words in parentheses.

1. David is (writing) _____ a check for new appliances.

2. He is (completing) _____ the check right now.

3. Ana and David have (contemplated) _____
   this purchase.

4. They have (discussed together) _____ the
   acquisition.

5. They discussed it (completely) _____ .

6. The old appliances (continue) _____ acting
   up.

7. Ana and David (carefully examined) _____
   their resources.

8. They considered the (positive and negative points) _____

   _____ of the purchase.

9. They even considered (not having) _____
   these items.

10. David and Ana (decided) _____
    to go for the trade-in option.

11. They'll be getting (items at a lower than usual price) _____

    _____ .

12. They're certainly (receiving the complete value for what they paid)

    _____ .

Exercise 3
Answer these questions orally.

1. Have you thought over purchasing new appliances?
2. Did you talk it over at length with anyone?
3. Why might you have to look into your savings account before making
   up your mind?
4. If your appliances keep on working, can you do without new ones?
5. What are some pros and cons of buying new appliances?
6. What might be a good buy for a new washer?

7. What does it mean if you say, "I certainly got my money's worth on that deal!"?

8. What's the difference between writing out a check and making out a check?

Exercise 4

Match the idiom to its definition by writing the letter of the definition on the line next to the idiom number.

1. _____ a good buy   a. to continue

2. _____ to talk over   b. thoroughly

3. _____ pros and cons   c. to discuss together

4. _____ to keep on   d. to think about

5. _____ to make up one's mind   e. to forgo

6. _____ to get one's money's worth   f. to complete

     g. to decide

7. _____ at length

     h. to get complete value for the price paid

8. _____ to write out

9. _____ to make out   i. to examine carefully

10. _____ to think over   j. positive and negative points of an issue

11. _____ to look into

     k. a lower than usual price

12. _____ to do without

     l. to write in full

Exercise 5

Respond to these statements orally.

1. Name three items you can do without if you have no money.

2. Name some pros and cons of shopping with a credit card.

3. Name one appliance that keeps on acting up.

107

4. Name two stores you write checks out to.

5. Name one problem you have thought over.

6. Name one item you bought that was a good buy.

7. Give one problem you have thought over.

8. Give one reason for looking into your resources when purchasing something major.

Exercise 6
Underline the words in parentheses that best correspond to the italicized idioms.

1. They *keep on* having good luck. They (continue, consider, begin) having good luck.

2. We contemplated the matter *at length*. We contemplated it (briefly, well, superficially).

3. We *talked over* the situation. We (discussed, continued, ignored) the situation.

4. He must *look into* his resources before buying expensive items. He must (ignore, consider, overlook) his resources.

5. David considered the *pros and cons* of getting an electric saw. He considered the (negative, positive, positive and negative) points of getting an electric saw.

6. She *makes up her mind* alone. She (makes her own decisions, discusses her thoughts, talks about her problems).

7. He is *writing out* a check. He is (reading, writing, memorizing) a check.

8. Ana will *make out* a list of necessary items. She will (discuss, talk about, write) the list.

9. She *thought over* the purchase. She (contemplated, discussed, hardly considered) the purchase.

10. It was *a good buy*. It was (a lower than usual, a higher than usual, the usual) price.

11. We can *do without* a new toaster. We (have to have, need, don't need) a new toaster.

12. You can really *get your money's worth* at that store! You can really get (complete value, incomplete value, some money) at that store!

Exercise 7
Reread the dialogue. Tell the story in your own words using the idioms.

Exercise 8

Complete the second sentence by substituting idioms for the italicized words.

1. They consider that refrigerator to be *at a lower than usual price.*

   They consider that refrigerator to be _____ .

2. He will *write* a check for the full amount.

   He will _____ a check for the full amount.

3. We discussed the *positive and negative aspects* of the purchase for several days.

   We discussed the _____ of the purchase for several days.

4. David and Ana always *discuss* their plans *with each other.*

   David and Ana always _____ their plans.

5. They *continue* advertising their new products.

   They _____ advertising their new products.

6. If you compare prices, it's easier *to get full value for what you pay.*

   If you compare prices, it's easier _____ .

7. We *decided* to compare prices for washing machines.

   We _____ to compare prices for washing machines.

8. We compared the various prices *carefully.*

   We compared the various prices _____ .

9. They *contemplated* charging some of the appliances.

   They _____ charging some of the appliances.

10. They decided *to forgo* some items.

    They decided _____ some items.

11. We *carefully examined* both the quality and the prices of the various appliances.

We _____ both the quality and the prices of the various appliances.

12. She is *writing* a list of the prices.

She is _____ a list of the prices.

Exercise 9
Change these sentences to the third person singular. Use *he* or *she* as indicated.

Example: *We were* tired out after *our* trip.

(He) ___*He was*___ tired out after ___*his*___ trip.

1. *They thought their* decision over.

(She) _____ decision over.

2. *We looked* into *our* finances.

(He) _____ into _____ finances.

3. *I will make* out the price list *my* way.

(He) _____ out the price list _____ way.

4. *They must do* without those things.

(She) _____ without those things.

5. *Are you writing* out a check from *your* personal account?

(She) _____ out a check from _____ personal account?

6. *My* appliances keep on breaking down, and *I don't know* what to do.

   (She) _____ appliances keep on breaking down, and _____

   _____ what to do.

7. There are too many pros and cons for *us* to consider.

   There are too many pros and cons for (he) _____ to consider.

8. *I made* up *my* mind before entering the store.

   (He) _____ up _____ mind before entering the store.

9. *David and Ana hope* to get a good buy on *their* purchases.

   (She) _____ to get a good buy on _____

   _____ purchases.

10. *I didn't get my* money's worth on that order.

    (He) _____ money's worth on that order.

11. *We talk* over *our* problems with the counselor.

    (She) _____ over _____
    problems with the counselor.

12. *Do they have* to think about it at length?

    (He) _____ to think about it at length?

Exercise 10
Complete the idiom phrase in each sentence.

1. We knew we had a good _____ on that purchase, so we took it.

2. They talked it _____ for many hours before making up their minds.

111

3. When you write _____ the check, please write legibly.

4. They kept _____ looking in every store until they found what they wanted.

5. We must understand the _____ and cons of buying a house in the city.

6. When you make _____ the list, don't forget to add oatmeal and raisins.

7. We already discussed it at _____ , so I don't want to talk about it anymore.

8. Let's look _____ the possibility of leasing a car instead of buying one. Maybe it will be cheaper.

9. I can easily do _____ a bigger TV. The one I have is fine.

10. When will you give me your decision? You've been thinking it _____

    _____ for a week.

11. It's hard to _____ _____ my mind when there are so many choices.

12. Even if I get _____ money's _____ , that car is still too expensive to buy.

Exercise 11
With a partner, create and perform an interesting, funny, enjoyable dialogue. Use as many idioms from this lesson as possible.

Exercise 12
Write sentences with the idioms given.

1. to do without

   _____

2. to write out (write the sentence in two ways)

   _____

   _____

3. a good buy

_____

4. to look into

_____

5. at length

_____

6. to make up one's mind

_____

7. to talk over (write the sentences in two ways)

_____

_____

8. to keep on

_____

Exercise 13
Circle the letter of the sentence that corresponds to the idiom used in the numbered sentence.

1. She made up her mind to improve her education.
   a. She decided to improve her education.
   b. There's a possibility she'll improve her education.
   c. She might improve her education.
2. The counselor wrote the camp regulations out.
   a. The counselor failed to write the camp regulations.
   b. The counselor considered writing the camp regulations.
   c. The counselor finished writing the camp regulations.
3. They looked into their family problems.
   a. They knew exactly what to do about their problems.
   b. They examined the cause of their problems.
   c. They pretended their problems didn't exist.

4. We talked over moving to another city.

    a. We moved to another city.

    b. We bought a house in another city.

    c. We discussed moving to another city.

5. His stamp collection was an excellent buy.

    a. He got an excellent stamp collection for too much money.

    b. He didn't pay too much for the stamp collection.

    c. He paid a high price for the stamp collection.

6. Let's do without the dessert.

    a. Let's eat the dessert.

    b. Let's consider eating the dessert.

    c. Let's not eat the dessert.

7. Because he had no money, he thought over fixing the car by himself.

    a. He discussed fixing the car by himself.

    b. He considered fixing the car by himself.

    c. He talked about fixing the car by himself.

8. He got his money's worth on his college education.

    a. He received a good education.

    b. He paid too much for his college education.

    c. His education was questionable.

9. There are many pros and cons to having your own business.

    a. There are good reasons for having your own business.

    b. There are positive and negative aspects to having your own business.

    c. There are many benefits to having your own business.

10. They made the registration forms out.

    a. They completed the forms with the proper information.

    b. They planned to read the forms later.

    c. They discussed the forms at length.

11. It kept on raining every day while we were at the beach.

    a. It rained periodically.

    b. It rained occasionally.

    c. It rained continuously.

12. They considered her credentials at length.

    a. They carefully considered her credentials.

    b. They superficially considered her credentials.

    c. They hardly considered her credentials.

Exercise 14
Complete the following exercise by using *by* and the correct reflexive:
myself, yourself, himself, herself, itself, ourselves, yourselves, themselves.

Example: I came to the United States *by myself* .
I came to the United States *alone.*

1. She prepared dinner _____ . She did it with no one's help.

2. I fixed my car _____ . No one else helped me.

3. The children went to the store _____ . No one else went with them.

4. You should all answer these questions _____ . Don't ask others for assistance.

5. We painted the house _____ . We were able to do it without anyone's help.

6. Clean up your room _____ . Do it alone.

7. The bird built its nest _____ . Only that bird gathered the twigs and grass.

8. He went out in the canoe _____ . He was the only one in the canoe.

9. The young cubs searched for food _____ . No other animals went with them.

10. She'll decide _____ . Don't tell her what to do.

Lesson 9

Putting Our Heads Together

Ana: I'm glad we're finally *fixing up* our apartment. It's beginning to feel like home.

David: I'm glad, too. We've certainly put in a lot of time thinking over how we want to redecorate it.

Ana: Yes, but now that we are *about to do over* the living room, we'll have *to come up with* some good ways *to cut costs.*

David: Well, if we *put our heads together,* we'll *figure out* something.

Ana: I plan on taking advantage of my sewing abilities and making drapes *to go with* the new decor we're planning.

David: And I've made up my mind *to put up* new bookshelves that I can make *on my own.*

Ana: We can also stop in at Mike's Wayside Furniture and see what they have to offer. I've heard they have an excellent selection of furnishings for sale.

David: They do. How about going soon? There's a special sale *going on* where all living room furniture is *on sale* for up to 30 percent off.

Ana: Well, it sounds like we'll be making out pretty well.

David: Between using our own skills and getting good buys, we should have it made!

Definitions

to fix up: to redecorate, to refurnish, to remodel, to do over
Ana is fixing up the kitchen. She is redecorating it.

about to: planning or preparing to do immediately, ready to
Are you about to go to the store? Are you ready to go?

to do over: to redecorate, to refurnish, to remodel, to fix up
They are doing the dining room over. They are redecorating it.

to come up with: to create, to originate, to suggest, to find
Who came up with these beautiful designs? Who created them?

to cut costs: to reduce spending
We're learning to cut costs. We're learning to reduce our spending.

to put (your, their, our) heads together: to ask each other's advice, to discuss or consult jointly
They put their heads together to solve the problem. They tried to solve the problem by consulting each other.

to figure out: to find an answer or a way, to solve
They figured out how to redecorate cheaply. They found a way to redecorate cheaply.

to go with: to match, to correspond, to harmonize
The designs go with each other. They match each other.

to put up: to build, to erect, to hang, to suspend
Where can we put the paintings up? Where can we hang them?

on one's own: alone, without assistance
Did they build the house on their own? Did they build it without assistance from others?

to go on: to occur, to happen, to continue
There's a big sale going on at the mall. There's a big sale happening at the mall.

on sale: at a reduced price
All drapery is on sale this week. All drapery is at a reduced price.

The following idioms may be separated by the object. These idioms may be said in two ways:

to fix up:

We must fix up this house.

We must fix this house up.

to do over:

They will do over the bedroom.

They will do the bedroom over.

to figure out:

We figured out the problem.

We figured the problem out.

to put up:

He put up the shelves.

He put the shelves up.

Exercise 1

Answer these questions from the dialogue orally.

1. What are David and Ana fixing up?
2. What are they about to do over?
3. Why do you think they'll have to come up with ways to cut costs?
4. How might putting their heads together help them figure out how to cut costs?
5. What will go with the drapes that Ana plans on making?
6. What has David made up his mind to put up?
7. Why will he make them on his own?
8. Where is there a furniture special going on?
9. What kind of furniture is on sale?

Exercise 2

Write the idioms from the dialogue that correspond to the words in parentheses.

1. David and Ana are (redecorating) _____ their home.

2. They are (planning to immediately) _____ refurnish the living room.

3. They intend (to redecorate) _____ the room without spending a lot of money.

4. They will (find) _____ ways to reduce costs.

5. They will find ways (to reduce spending) _____ .

6. Ana and David must (consult with each other) _____ .

7. They will (solve) _____ which way to turn.

8. She wants the drapes (to match) _____ the new decor they're planning.

9. David has made up his mind (to build) _____ bookshelves.

10. He can make them (alone) _____ .

11. There is a special sale (occurring) _____ at Mike's Wayside Furniture.

12. All living room furniture is (at a reduced price) _____ .

Exercise 3
Answer these questions orally.

1. Do you enjoy fixing your home up? Explain.
2. Are there any rooms you are about to do over?
3. Do you enjoy putting up new decorations?
4. Can you do it on your own?
5. Do you and your spouse, or friend, put your heads together for new ideas? Explain.
6. What kind of ideas might you come up with?
7. What kind of furnishings go with the decor you prefer?
8. How might you figure out ways to cut costs?
9. Do you know of any place that has a furniture sale going on?
10. What kind of furnishings might you buy on sale?

Exercise 4
Match the idiom to its definition by writing the letter of the definition on the line next to the idiom number.

1. _____ to go with   a. to reduce spending

2. _____ to put up   b. to redecorate

3. _____ to fix up   c. to solve

4. _____ on one's own   d. to originate

5. _____ on sale   e. to discuss jointly

6. _____ to cut costs   f. to refurnish

7. _____ about to   g. ready to

8. _____ to figure out   h. to occur

9. _____ to do over   i. at a reduced price

10. _____ to come up with   j. without assistance

11. _____ to go on   k. to match

12. _____ to put...heads   l. to hang
         together

Exercise 5
Respond to these statements orally.

1. Give three ways to fix the kitchen up.
2. Give two places to put bookshelves up.
3. Give one way to cut costs when shopping.
4. Name two items you have bought on sale.
5. Name one place that has a drapery sale going on.
6. Name two items that go with your furniture.
7. Name one item you can make on your own.

Exercise 6
Underline the words in parentheses that best correspond to the italicized idioms.

1. When they *put their heads together,* they find the solution quickly. They find the solution through (discussion, meditation, argument).

2. The decorator *came up with* beautiful color schemes. He (remodeled, originated, reduced) the color schemes.

3. They were able *to cut costs* when they built their house. They were able to (redecorate it, reduce spending, create their own decor).

4. Ana bought the new accessories *on sale.* She bought them at (a higher than usual, a lower than usual, the regular) price.

5. The colors *go with* each other. They (clash, harmonize, differ).

6. We will *do over* the bedroom soon. We will (destroy, demolish, remodel) the bedroom.

7. David is *putting up* new doors. He is (hanging, removing, storing) the doors.

8. He is *about to* paint the ceiling. He is going to paint it (now, tomorrow, next week).

9. We want *to fix up* the kitchen. We want to (make no changes, do it over, keep it as it is).

10. They *figured out* how to fix the plumbing. They (found a way, didn't know how, had no idea how) to fix the plumbing.

11. The sale *went on* for two weeks. The sale (was discontinued, continued, was considered) for two weeks.

12. I did it *on my own.* I did it (with everybody's help, without anybody's help, with my family).

Exercise 7
Reread the dialogue. Tell the story in your own words using the idioms.

Exercise 8
Complete the second sentence by substituting idioms for the italicized words.

1. Which color *matches* brown?

   Which color _____ brown?

2. Wallpaper is *at a reduced price* this week.

   Wallpaper is _____ this week.

3. We can *refurnish* the living room next year.

   We can _____ the living room next year.

4. They are *planning to* begin *immediately.*

   They are _____ begin.

5. It will be expensive *to redecorate* both rooms.

   It will be expensive _____ both rooms.

6. When will you *hang* the curtains?

   When will you _____ the curtains?

7. If he tries, he will be able to do it *alone.*

   If he tries, he will be able to do it _____ .

8. Let's *ask each other's advice* more often.

   Let's _____ more often.

9. They have to *reduce spending* because they don't have much money.

   They have to _____ because they don't have much money.

10. Their going out of business sale is *occurring* right now.

    Their going out of business sale is _____ right now.

11. He *found* the answer to the problem.

    He _____ the answer to the problem.

12. They finally *found a way* to save more money.

    They finally _____ how to save more money.

Exercise 9
Change these sentences to questions.

Example: *She wrote* out the check.

_____*Did she write*_____ out the check?

1. *They have cut* costs on their remodeling project.

_____ costs on their remodeling project?

2. *We fixed* up the house last summer.

_____ up the house last summer?

3. *They prefer* buying their furnishings on sale.

_____ buying their furnishings on sale?

4. *David will put* up the kitchen cabinets.

_____ up the kitchen cabinets?

5. *I can* do it on my own.

_____ do it on my own?

6. *She figured* out the size of the living room carpet.

_____ out the size of the living room carpet?

7. *They put* their heads together for all their problems.

_____ their heads together for all their problems?

8. *The remodeling project has been* going on all summer.

_____ going on all summer?

9. *Ana is* about to choose the colors.

_____ about to choose the colors?

10. *They won't* do over the kitchen.

_____ do over the kitchen?

11. *It would have gone* nicely with the new decor.

_____ nicely with the new decor?

12. *The architect came* up with an innovative idea.

_____ up with an innovative idea?

Exercise 10
Complete the idiom phrase in each sentence.

1. He put _____ pictures and paintings on two walls in every room.

2. There's a great sale going _____ . Everything is so cheap!

3. I bought the television _____ sale. It was less than half the price.

4. They put _____ heads _____ for almost every decision. They want each other's advice.

5. I like to do many things on _____ _____ . It's often easier to work alone.

6. I don't think the drapes go _____ the carpet. The colors clash.

7. We need to do _____ the cabinets. The wood has lost its shine.

8. She's about _____ leave. She's already late for her appointment.

9. I couldn't figure _____ which way to turn, so I did nothing.

10. If you come _____ _____ a good idea, let me know. We need to find a good way to handle this situation.

11. Let's fix ＿＿＿＿＿＿ the house before we sell it. It will be easier to sell if it's in very good condition.

12. We should try to cut ＿＿＿＿＿＿ on our weekly bills. We need to save more money.

Exercise 11
With a partner, create and perform an interesting, funny, enjoyable dialogue. Use as many idioms from this lesson as possible.

Exercise 12
Write sentences with the idioms given.

1. to cut costs

＿＿＿＿＿＿＿＿＿＿＿＿＿＿＿＿＿＿＿＿＿＿＿＿＿＿＿

2. on one's own

＿＿＿＿＿＿＿＿＿＿＿＿＿＿＿＿＿＿＿＿＿＿＿＿＿＿＿

3. to go with

＿＿＿＿＿＿＿＿＿＿＿＿＿＿＿＿＿＿＿＿＿＿＿＿＿＿＿

4. to figure out (write the sentence in two ways)

＿＿＿＿＿＿＿＿＿＿＿＿＿＿＿＿＿＿＿＿＿＿＿＿＿＿＿

＿＿＿＿＿＿＿＿＿＿＿＿＿＿＿＿＿＿＿＿＿＿＿＿＿＿＿

5. to fix up (write the sentence in two ways)

＿＿＿＿＿＿＿＿＿＿＿＿＿＿＿＿＿＿＿＿＿＿＿＿＿＿＿

＿＿＿＿＿＿＿＿＿＿＿＿＿＿＿＿＿＿＿＿＿＿＿＿＿＿＿

6. about to

＿＿＿＿＿＿＿＿＿＿＿＿＿＿＿＿＿＿＿＿＿＿＿＿＿＿＿

7. to come up with

_____

8. on sale

_____

Exercise 13

Circle the letter of the sentence that corresponds to the idiom used in the numbered sentence.

1. They do over the store before every holiday.
   a. They leave it as it is.
   b. They put up decorations.
   c. They make no changes.

2. They figured out how many days it would take them to drive to Alaska.
   a. They calculated the time.
   b. They reduced the costs by driving to Alaska.
   c. They miscalculated the time.

3. His friend is about to leave for the library.
   a. She has already left.
   b. She will leave in a few hours.
   c. She is leaving now.

4. The doctors put their heads together to find a cure for the disease.
   a. They didn't discuss a cure for the disease.
   b. They were too busy to discuss a cure for the disease.
   c. They talked about a cure for the disease.

5. To cut costs, they had a very small wedding.
   a. They tried to maximize expenses.
   b. After the wedding, they thought about the costs.
   c. They tried to minimize expenses.

6. The brown shoes go with the suit.
   a. The colors contrast.
   b. The colors are compatible.
   c. The colors differ.

7. They put a monument up to honor Abraham Lincoln.

   a. They removed a monument.

   b. They desecrated a monument.

   c. They erected a monument.

8. He became a rich man on his own.

   a. He became rich by inheriting money.

   b. He became rich by working hard.

   c. He became rich by asking others for help.

9. The chemist came up with a new medicine.

   a. He discovered a new medicine.

   b. He tried a new medicine.

   c. He rejected a new medicine.

10. They fixed the old buildings up.

   a. They destroyed them.

   b. They burned them.

   c. They improved them.

11. They were excited when they saw the items they wanted on sale.

   a. The items were too expensive.

   b. The items cost more than they expected.

   c. The items were a good buy.

12. There's a New Year's party going on at 54 Grand Street.

   a. The New Year's party will be starting soon.

   b. They're still celebrating the New Year.

   c. They're going to have a party to celebrate the New Year.

Exercise 14

Use either *for* or *ago* in the following sentences.

Example: We have been in the United States *for* five months.
        (*for precedes* a duration of time)
        We came to the United States five months ago.
        (*ago*, meaning *in the past*, *follows* a duration of time)

1. I haven't seen you _____ a long time.

   I saw you last a long time _____ .

2. She started studying two years _____ .

   She has been studying _____ two years.

3. They got married a month _____ .

   They've been married _____ one month.

4. He went shopping an hour _____ .

   He's been shopping _____ an hour.

5. The television has needed repairs _____ a long time.

   The television began needing repairs a long time _____ .

6. Cars cost less some years _____ .

   Cars haven't cost less _____ some years.

7. Some months _____ , she began having problems.

   _____ some months, she's been having problems.

8. The door was locked twenty minutes _____ .

   The door has been locked _____ twenty minutes.

9. He's been at the beach _____ a few days.

   He went to the beach a few days _____ .

10. They finished college a month _____ .

    They've been out of college _____ a month.

Running Out of Just About Everything

Ana: I have to do our grocery shopping **on the run**, David. I'm **in a hurry**, and I plan on doing my errands very quickly.

David: Did you make out a list **in advance** for the items we need **to pick up**?

Ana: I certainly did, and I'm looking it over trying **to keep in mind** each item.

David: Well, I know we've **run out** of garlic and onions, and we seem to be **running short** of **just about** everything else.

Ana: I know. While I **pick out** some tender lean veal in the meat department, how about your getting the garlic and onions in the produce department?

David: Sounds good to me. And since I'll be going past the bakery section, why don't I pick up some of those **mouth-watering** pastries we're so **crazy about**?

Ana: I don't know about that, David. Maybe we should do without those tempting morsels. We've been trying so hard to **cut down** on fat and calories!

David: Perhaps you're right, Ana. I'll forget about it this time.

Ana: Let me just go over my list again, David, and I'll meet you at the register shortly.

David: Great. Then we can be off to our other errands.

Definitions

on the run: doing things quickly, acting in a hurried manner, rushing
  She's doing her shopping on the run. She's doing it quickly.

in a hurry: doing things quickly, acting in a hurried manner, rushing
  Why are you always in a hurry? Why are you always rushing?

in advance (of):   beforehand, before, before doing something
  She made out her list in advance. She made it out before going to the store.

to pick up: to buy, to purchase, to get
  I'll pick up a few groceries at the store. I'll purchase them.

to keep in mind: to remember, to think about
  Can you keep all the items in mind? Can you remember them all?

to run out (of):   to have no more, to consume completely
  They ran out of bread. They have no more bread.

to run short (of):   to have less than enough, not to have enough, lacking sufficient supply
  We are running short of flour. We don't have enough flour.

just about: almost, nearly
  I've just about finished my shopping. I've almost finished my shopping.

to pick out: to choose, to select
  They picked out the leanest meat. They selected the leanest meat.

to be crazy about: to like something or someone very much, to be very attracted to
  Are you crazy about pizza? Do you like pizza very much?

mouth-watering: exceptionally delicious, appealing to the senses
  This dessert is mouth-watering! It tastes very delicious!

to cut down (on):   to decrease, to lessen, to reduce
  They try to cut down on red meat. They try to eat less red meat.

The following idioms may be separated by the object. These idioms may be said in two ways:

to pick up:
>   She picked up fresh carrots.
>   She picked fresh carrots up.

to keep in mind:
>   We keep in mind our list.
>   We keep our list in mind.

to pick out:
>   He picked out a dessert.
>   He picked a dessert out.

Exercise 1
Answer these questions from the dialogue orally.

1. Why is Ana doing her shopping on the run?
2. Is she in a hurry? Explain.
3. Why did Ana make out a list in advance for the items she needs to pick up?
4. How does she try to keep all the items in mind?
5. Which items have David and Ana run out of?
6. What does David mean by, "We seem to be running short of just about everything else"?
7. What does Ana pick out in the meat department?
8. What mouth-watering foods are David and Ana crazy about?
9. On what are David and Ana trying to cut down?

Exercise 2
Write the idioms from the dialogue that correspond to the words in parentheses.

1. Ana is doing the grocery shopping (quickly) _____ .

2. She is (rushing) _____ .

3. Ana made out a list (beforehand) _____ .

4. She plans (to buy) _____ items on her list.

5. She is trying (to remember) _____ each item.

6. David and Ana have (consumed completely) _____ of garlic and onions.

7. They seem to be (lacking sufficient supply) _____ of other foods.

8. They seem to be lacking (almost) _____ all other foods.

9. Ana (selects) _____ tender lean veal in the meat department.

10. David would like to get some (exceptionally delicious) _____

_____ pastries.

11. David and Ana (like very much) _____ pastries.

12. They are trying (to eat less) _____ on fat and calories.

Exercise 3
Answer these questions orally.

1. When do you do your shopping on the run?
2. Do you enjoy shopping when you are in a hurry? Explain.
3. How does having a list made out in advance help you in your shopping?
4. In what ways do you try to keep the items in mind?
5. How many times a week do you pick groceries up?
6. Which store do you go to when you run short of food?
7. Which foods do you frequently run out of?
8. What types of food are you crazy about?
9. Do you try to cut down on fat and calories when you pick out food?
10. Is there a particular food that you find mouth-watering? Explain.

Exercise 4

Match the idiom to its definition by writing the letter of the definition on the line next to the idiom number.

1. _____ just about   a. to select

2. _____ to cut down   b. doing things quickly

3. _____ to keep in mind   c. rushing

4. _____ to run short   d. to reduce

5. _____ to pick out   e. to like very much

6. _____ in a hurry   f. to remember

7. _____ mouth-watering   g. to purchase

8. _____ on the run   h. beforehand

9. _____ to pick up   i. almost

10. _____ to be crazy about   j. to have less than enough

11. _____ to run out   k. tasting exceptionally good

12. _____ in advance   l. to have no more

Exercise 5

Respond to these statements orally.

1. Name four items you occasionally run out of.
2. Name two items you pick out in the produce department.
3. Name one food you ran short of last week.
4. Name two foods you are crazy about.
5. Name one place to purchase mouth-watering foods.
6. Give one way to cut down on your food bill.
7. Give two reasons for making out a list in advance of shopping.
8. Give one place to pick up farm-fresh eggs.

Exercise 6
Underline the words in parentheses that best correspond to the italicized idioms.

1. She *picked out* the best one. She (didn't choose, selected, couldn't find) the best one.

2. The chef is *running short* of Chinese noodles. He (has a sufficient supply of, doesn't have enough, has enough) Chinese noodles.

3. They are eating their lunch *in a hurry.* They are eating (slowly, quickly, leisurely).

4. This delicacy is *mouth-watering.* It is (tasty, tasteless, watery).

5. They *cut down* on all their purchases. They (increased, reduced, continued) their purchases.

6. I *ran out* of flour and eggs. I (never use, have enough, don't have any) flour and eggs.

7. I bought *just about* all the items we need. I bought (everything, almost everything, nothing) we need.

8. We *are crazy about* most vegetables. We (abhor, like, dislike) them.

9. She tries *to keep in mind* the entire list. She tries to (forget, write, remember) the list.

10. He is *on the run* from morning until night. He (hurries, relaxes, procrastinates).

11. They discussed the items they needed to purchase *in advance* of shopping. They discussed them (after, during, before) shopping.

12. Don't forget *to pick up* milk at the dairy, please! Don't forget to (sell, drink, get) milk.

Exercise 7
Reread the dialogue. Tell the story in your own words using the idioms.

Exercise 8
Complete the second sentence by substituting idioms for the italicized words.

1. He was *almost* ready to leave when the phone rang.

   He was _____ ready to leave when the phone rang.

2. She checked her money *before* deciding what to do.

She checked her money _____ of deciding what to do.

3. They try *to remember* everything at the same time.

They try _____ everything at the same time.

4. She did it *quickly*.

She did it _____ .

5. They *are attracted to* delicious-looking pastries.

They _____ delicious-looking pastries.

6. Why did you *choose* that brand of butter?

Why did you _____ that brand of butter?

7. I *didn't have any more* money.

I _____ of money.

8. Where can you *buy* fish?

Where can you _____ fish?

9. They found *exceptionally tasty* delicacies at the shop.

They found _____ delicacies at the shop.

10. We *reduce* our expenses by purchasing items on sale.

We _____ on our expenses by purchasing items on sale.

11. She is *going quickly* when she has shopping to do.

She is _____ when she has shopping to do.

12. They *didn't have enough* food for their guests.

They _____ of food for their guests.

Exercise 9
Make these sentences negative by using the negative word indicated.

Example: He *waited* for the bus to arrive.

(not) He _ *didn't wait* _ for the bus to arrive.

1. They *always pick* out the most expensive dinner.

   (never) They _____ out the most expensive
   dinner.

2. He *picks* his evening groceries up at the local store.

   (not) He _____ his evening groceries up at
   the local store.

3. They *are* crazy about Oriental food.

   (not) They _____ crazy about Oriental food.

4. We *often run* out of food.

   (seldom) We _____ out of food.

5. They *plan* their dinners in advance.

   (rarely) They _____ their dinners in advance.

6. He *has learned* to cut down on rich foods.

   (not) He _____ to cut down on rich foods.

7. He *is always* in a hurry.

   (seldom) He _____ in a hurry.

8. She *frequently forgets* her shopping list when she shops on the run.

   (never) She _____ her shopping list when she
   shops on the run.

9. It *was* just about 7:30 when she left.

   (not) It _____ just about 7:30 when she left.

10. It *was* a mouth-watering dinner.

(hardly) It _____ a mouth-watering dinner.

11. We *ran* short of sugar when we were making a cake.

(not) We _____ short of sugar when we were
making a cake.

12. She *keeps* in mind all the errands she has to do.

(rarely) She _____ in mind all the errands
she has to do.

Exercise 10
Complete the idiom phrase in each sentence.

1. We have run _____ of lasagna. Now some people won't get
any.

2. I was in such a _____ , I forgot my purse.

3. He's crazy _____ all kinds of desserts and eats much too
much.

4. We were just _____ to leave when they telephoned us.

5. You really did pick _____ the best meat! It's lean and
delicious.

6. We can have a New Year's party if you want; but we have to discuss

it _____ advance.

7. You have so many things to remember, how can you keep everything

_____ _____ ?

8. We always seem to run _____ of our basic foods, yet we
always make it through the week.

9. Of course, it's easy to forget to do some things when you're always

on the _____ .

10. Pick _____ plenty of fruit since we don't know how much we will need.

11. This tastes better than I imagined! It is absolutely _____ -watering!

12. If you cut _____ _____ calories, you'll lose weight.

Exercise 11
With a partner, create and perform an interesting, funny, enjoyable dialogue. Use as many idioms from this lesson as possible.

Exercise 12
Write sentences with the idioms given.

1. to cut down (on)

_____

2. in a hurry

_____

3. just about

_____

4. to run out (of)

_____

5. to pick out (write the sentence in two ways)

_____

_____

6. to pick up (write the sentence in two ways)

_____

_____

7. to be crazy about

_____

8. on the run

_____

Exercise 13

Circle the letter of the sentence that corresponds to the idiom used in the numbered sentence.

1. We ran short of money and couldn't continue our trip.

   a. We had enough money.

   b. We didn't have enough money.

   c. We had more than enough money.

2. They bought the tickets three weeks in advance of leaving for Japan.

   a. They left for Japan three weeks early.

   b. They advanced their trip to Japan by three weeks.

   c. They got their tickets three weeks before leaving for Japan.

3. He is crazy about his new girlfriend.

   a. He does crazy things for her.

   b. His girlfriend is crazy.

   c. He loves her.

4. She picked out the man she's going to marry.

   a. She doesn't want to marry.

   b. She isn't sure whom she will marry.

   c. She knows exactly whom she will marry.

5. They kept in mind the rules and regulations of the camping grounds.

   a. They forgot the rules and regulations.

   b. They failed to remember the rules and regulations.

   c. They didn't forget the rules and regulations.

6. The mouth-watering pies at the bakery were selling fast.

   a. The pies were delicious.

   b. The pies were stale.

   c. The pies were tasteless.

7. Because she was on the run, she forgot her keys.

    a. Because she was running, she forgot her keys.

    b. Because she was exercising, she forgot her keys.

    c. Because she was rushing, she forgot her keys.

8. They went roller skating just about every Saturday night.

    a. They went skating every Saturday night.

    b. They occasionally went skating on Saturday nights.

    c. They went skating most Saturday nights.

9. He was in a hurry because it was late.

    a. He was dallying.

    b. He was rushing.

    c. He was relaxing.

10. We ran out of gas on the highway.

    a. The gas tank was empty.

    b. The gas tank was half empty.

    c. The gas tank was nearly full.

11. He cut down on his working hours because he wasn't getting enough sleep.

    a. He began working more hours.

    b. He began working less hours.

    c. He was sleeping too much.

12. She picked her costume up at The Costume Shop.

    a. She designed the costume.

    b. She made the costume.

    c. She bought the costume.

Exercise 14

Use the correct object pronouns in the following sentences (*me, you, him, her, it, us, you, them*).

Example: I see *Mike* daily.

I see ___*him*___ daily.

1. We saw *many animals* at the circus.

    We saw _____ at the circus.

2. When it began to rain, we put *the tools* in the garage.

   When it began to rain, we put _____ in the garage.

3. They want *Jim and me* to go with them.

   They want _____ to go with them.

4. He saw *a lovely girl* in the park.

   He saw _____ in the park.

5. I saw *your sister and you* at the shopping mall.

   I saw _____ at the shopping mall.

6. She wants *her father* to read her a story.

   She wants _____ to read her a story.

7. He put *a flower* in her hair.

   He put _____ in her hair.

8. Our relatives invited *Ariana, Dahlia, and me* to visit them in California.

   Our relatives invited _____ to visit them in California.

9. When she was talking to Ken, she asked, "Can I go to the beach

   with _____ ?"

10. Ken replied, "I'd love to have you come with _____ .
    You're my favorite little niece."

Review of Lessons 6–10

Exercise 1
Write the correct form of the best idiom for each italicized definition.
Use each idiom once.

to put money into	on one's last legs
to put . . . heads together	out of this world
in advance	to sound like
how about	to look into
to go out	to bend over backwards
to take a break	at length
to call in	to act up
to go with	to keep in mind
to run short	on sale
to pick up	up against

1. By *consulting each other,* they found the solution to the math problem.

   By _____ , they found the solution to the math problem.

2. We enjoy *going somewhere for entertainment* every Saturday night.

   We enjoy _____ every Saturday night.

3. They analyzed the information *carefully.*

   They analyzed the information _____ .

4. We have *to remember* all the things we must do before leaving.

   We have _____ all the things we must do before leaving.

5. I *didn't have enough* money, so I couldn't buy the dress.

   I _____ of money, so I couldn't buy the dress.

6. She knew it *beforehand*.

   She knew it _____ .

7. He *puts much effort into* pleasing his customers.

   He _____ to please his customers.

8. She bought her complete wardrobe *at a reduced price*.

   She bought her complete wardrobe _____ .

9. He is ill and has been *failing* for the past month.

   He is ill and has been _____ for the past month.

10. We need to *rest for a short time* from this tedious job.

    We need to _____ from this tedious job.

11. If the lawn mower *doesn't operate properly,* we'll have it repaired.

    If the lawn mower _____ , we'll have it repaired.

12. That performance was *fantastic!*

    That performance was _____ !

13. I *bought* the stained glass at an auction.

    I _____ the stained glass at an auction.

14. Don't *spend money* on that vehicle!

    Don't _____ that vehicle!

15. They *considered* alternative methods of saving their money.

    They _____ alternative methods of saving their money.

16. It *seems like* she's very excited about the Caribbean cruise.

It _____ she's very excited about the Caribbean cruise.

17. What design *matches* this?

What design _____ this?

18. Let's *telephone* for our dinner.

Let's _____ for our dinner.

19. He was *confronted with* the difficult decision of choosing between two jobs.

He was _____ the difficult decision of choosing between two jobs.

20. *What do you think of* going to the new Fine Arts Museum?

_____ going to the new Fine Arts Museum?

Exercise 2
Choose the idiom in parentheses that best completes the sentence.

1. When I _____ the check, I wrote the incorrect amount of money. (put money into, made out, looked over)

2. Before going on a cruise, we _____ every detail. (think over, run out of, pick up)

3. They _____ on that business venture. (on sale, on the run, got their money's worth)

4. It was an absolutely _____ restaurant! (how about, top-notch, on the run)

5. The students who took the test _____ failed to do well. (in a hurry, at length, about to)

6. They were happy to get _____ on their new furnishings. (mouth-watering, on sale, a good buy)

7. He _____ waving to us from the train.
   (worked out, settled on, kept on)

8. The heavy snowfall _____ all the airplanes at
   the airport. (sounded like, tied up, traded in)

9. She _____ a fantastic idea for recycling used
   items. (came up with, made up her mind, traded in)

10. She didn't know which dress _____ because
    all of them were beautiful. (to tie up, to work out, to pick out)

11. We decided _____ our problems together
    before deciding what to do. (to go with, to talk over, to do without)

12. After much debate, we finally _____
    vacationing at the seashore. (settled on, about to, went out)

13. They'll _____ a way to save enough money
    for a down payment on a new home. (cut costs, figure out, hold up)

14. The family _____ for many years, but now
    they want to have more and enjoy life. (worked out, settled on, did
    without)

15. The car _____ longer than we expected. (on
    its last legs, held up, tied up)

16. We plan _____ the entire house this coming
    year. (to wait on, to look into, to do over)

17. They _____ a beautiful building at the edge
    of town. (ate out, acted up, put up)

18. He _____ every detail of the report before
    submitting it. (traded in, went over, waited on)

19. We will _____ on everything if we need more
    money. (at length, do without, cut costs)

20. They will _____ the details of the party after
    they write the list. (work out, keep on, act up)

Exercise 3
Write the best idiom for each sentence. Use each idiom once.

just about	pros and cons
runs out	an arm and a leg
about to	writing out
to eat out	as hungry as a horse
make up her mind	to cut down
broke down	going on
crazy about	how about
to trade in	waits on
fixed up	on the run
on his own	mouth-watering

1. Kim was _____ leave the house when the telephone rang.

2. When the child saw all the delicious desserts, she couldn't _____

   _____ which one to choose.

3. They _____ the basement and now it is a cozy family room.

4. She didn't know where she had lost her ring, so she looked _____

   _____ everywhere in the house and yard.

5. Since he lost his job, they have had _____ on their food and clothing bills.

6. Lee's friend will give him money if he _____ of money before his vacation ends.

7. Sue eats breakfast _____ because she is always late for work.

8. The breakfront is a beautiful piece of furniture, but it costs _____

   _____ .

9. This _____ meal is a favorite of all customers.

10. The waitress _____ her customers courteously and efficiently.

11. Joe has been living _____ for many years and is accustomed to not having a family.

12. Jim wants _____ his old car for a motorcycle.

13. _____ going out to a good movie tonight?

14. When the car _____ , David had to walk to the nearest garage for help.

15. She is _____ the check for the proper amount of money.

16. She is _____ most Italian food.

17. After considering the _____ of remaining in New York City, he decided against it.

18. I haven't had a thing to eat all day! Now I'm _____

_____ .

19. There's a sale _____ at the downtown mall.

20. We like _____ at a fancy restaurant once every month.

Lesson 11

Catching the Flu

Ana: David, *what's the matter?* You look totally *wiped out.*

David: And that's exactly the way I feel. I don't know if I'm just *worn out* or if I'm really *coming down with* something.

Ana: Let me feel your head, David. Oh! You're *burning up!* You must be *running a temperature.*

David: I feel like I've *caught* the flu, Ana. My throat hurts, I feel dizzy, and I ache *from head to toe.*

Ana: Go lie down, David. You need to rest. Why don't I *call up* the doctor and make an appointment for this afternoon?

David: That sounds like a good idea. Once the doctor figures out what's wrong with me, he'll probably give me a prescription, tell me to drink lots of fluids, and want me to *take it easy.*

Ana: You're probably right. And if you follow the doctor's orders, you'll *be back on your feet* again *in no time at all.*

Definitions

what's the matter: what's the problem, what happened, what's wrong
  What's the matter with your arm? What happened to it?

151

wiped out: extremely exhausted, without energy, deeply fatigued

He was wiped out from his long illness. He felt extremely exhausted.

worn out: tired, exhausted, fatigued, with little energy

They were worn out after the three-hour test. They were exhausted after the test.

to come down with: to get or become sick with

The doctor came down with the flu. The doctor became sick with the flu.

burning up: very hot, having a high temperature

He's burning up! He has a very high temperature!

to run a temperature: to have a fever, to suffer from a fever

The child ran a temperature when he was ill. He had a fever.

to catch (an illness): to become ill with (a contagious disease)

She catches a cold every winter. She becomes ill with a cold every winter.

from head to toe: the complete body, throughout the entire body

Why do you ache from head to toe? Why does your complete body ache?

to call up: to telephone, to call on the telephone

He called up the doctor. He telephoned the doctor.

to take it easy: to relax, to rest, to enjoy leisure

When you're ill, you should take it easy. You should rest.

to be back on one's feet: to recover from an illness, to be better

After a week with the flu, he was back on his feet again. He was better after a week.

in no time at all: shortly, soon, in a short time

In no time at all, you'll be feeling fine. Soon you'll be feeling fine.

The following idiom may be separated by the object. This idiom may be said in two ways:

to call up:

He called up his friend.

He called his friend up.

Exercise 1

Answer these questions from the dialogue orally.

1. What's the matter with David, and why does he look wiped out?
2. Does David think he's worn out or really coming down with something?
3. Why does Ana say, "David, you're burning up!"?
4. Is David running a temperature?
5. Why does David think he's caught the flu?
6. How does he feel if he aches from head to toe?
7. Why does Ana call up the doctor?
8. Who will probably tell David to take it easy?
9. What does Ana mean when she says, "You'll be back on your feet again in no time at all!"?

Exercise 2

Write the idioms from the dialogue that correspond to the words in parentheses.

1. Ana asks David, "(What's wrong) _____ ?"

2. He looks totally (without energy) _____ .

3. Maybe he is just (tired) _____ .

4. Perhaps David is really (becoming sick with) _____ something.

5. Ana says, "Oh, David, you're (very hot) _____ !"

6. He must be (suffering from a fever) _____

   _____ .

7. David feels like he (became ill with) _____ the flu.

8. He aches (throughout his entire body) _____ .

9. Ana (telephones) _____ the doctor.

10. David will probably have to (rest) _____ .

11. David will (be better) _____
    soon.

12. David will be better (soon) _____ .

Exercise 3
Answer these questions orally.

1. How do you feel when you're coming down with something?
2. Do you usually ache from head to toe when you've caught the flu?
3. If you're burning up, are you usually running a temperature?
4. What's the difference between feeling wiped out and feeling worn out?
5. What might be the matter when you're very, very tired?
6. Do you need to call up the doctor when you're ill, or do you just take it easy on your own?
7. When you're ill, are you usually on your feet again in no time at all?

Exercise 4
Match the idiom to its definition by writing the letter of the definition on the line next to the idiom number.

1. _____ burning up

2. _____ in no time at all

3. _____ from head to toe

4. _____ what's the matter

5. _____ to run a temperature

6. _____ to catch (an illness)

7. _____ to call up

8. _____ worn out

9. _____ to be back on one's feet

a. to have a fever

b. extremely exhausted

c. to become ill with a contagious disease

d. to rest

e. soon

f. to become sick with

g. having a high fever

h. the complete body

i. what's the problem

10. _____ to take it easy   j. to telephone

11. _____ to come down with   k. to recover from an illness

12. _____ wiped out   l. tired

Exercise 5
Respond to these statements orally.

1. Name one doctor you call up when you're ill.
2. Name two illnesses a person can come down with.
3. Give one time you ached from head to toe.
4. Give the last time you caught a cold.
5. Give one time you ran a temperature in the past two years.
6. Give two ways to take it easy when you are ill.

Exercise 6
Underline the words in parentheses that best correspond to the italicized idioms.

1. He *took it easy* when he was sick. He (continued working, rested, failed to relax).
2. She was *worn out* after the operation. She was (fatigued, energetic, happy).
3. She is *back on her feet*! She is (becoming ill, not well, recovering).
4. The doctor said, "*Call me up* if you have any questions." The doctor said, "(Visit me, Telephone me, Don't bother me) if you have any questions."
5. All the children *came down with* the same disease. They (failed to get, got, recovered from) the same disease.
6. You're *burning up*! You're (very hot, recovering, exhausted)!
7. *In no time at all,* he was back at work. (Some time later, After a long time, Soon), he was back at work.
8. *What's the matter* with him? (What did he decide, What happened to him, Where did he go)?
9. The flu caused her to ache *from head to toe*. (Only her head, Only her toe, Her entire body) ached.
10. When he works very hard, he feels *wiped out*. He feels (good, relaxed, extremely tired).

155

11. You should rest when you *run a temperature*. You should rest when you (have a normal temperature, have a fever, feel well).

12. The child *caught a cold* after playing in the rain. After playing in the rain, he (improved, got a cold, was cold).

Exercise 7
Reread the dialogue. Tell the story in your own words using the idioms.

Exercise 8
Complete the second sentence by substituting idioms for the italicized words.

1. He was *extremely exhausted* all day long.

   He was _____ all day long.

2. She *became ill with* a cold after the ice skating party.

   She _____ a cold after the ice skating party.

3. The child *became sick with* the mumps.

   The child _____ the mumps.

4. His mother doesn't know *what's wrong* with him.

   His mother doesn't know _____
   with him.

5. He was covered with poison ivy *on his complete body*.

   He was covered with poison ivy _____ .

6. He feels *tired* when it's hot.

   He feels _____ when it's hot.

7. He was *very hot from fever* all afternoon.

   He was _____ all afternoon.

8. She's *recovered from her illness* and is returning to work.

   She's _____ and is returning to work.

9. *In a short time,* the children were running around again.

   _____ , the children were running around again.

10. Children often *have a fever* when they are ill.

    Children often _____ when they are ill.

11. She *telephoned* the dentist's office.

    She _____ the dentist's office.

12. He loves *to relax* all the time!

    He loves _____ all the time!

Exercise 9
Change the verbs in these sentences to contractions.

Example: *He is* off to the doctor's office.

_____*He's*_____ off to the doctor's office.

1. *He is* worn out and wants to rest.

   _____ worn out and wants to rest.

2. *What is* the matter with you?

   _____ the matter with you?

3. *He has been* running a temperature.

   _____ running a temperature.

4. *She will be* back on her feet.

   _____ back on her feet.

157

5. If *he had* taken it easy, *he would* have felt better.

   If _____ taken it easy, _____ have felt better.

6. They *cannot* move when they ache from head to toe.

   They _____ move when they ache from head to toe.

7. The child *has not* caught a cold all winter.

   The child _____ caught a cold all winter.

8. You *should not* feel so wiped out.

   You _____ feel so wiped out.

9. They *were not* burning up; they only had a mild fever.

   They _____ burning up; they only had a mild fever.

10. If they come down with the flu, they *will not* be able to go with us.

    If they come down with the flu, they _____ be able to go with us.

11. *Let us* call up the doctor and find out if he is in.

    _____ call up the doctor and find out if he is in.

12. *He will* be returning to work in no time at all.

    _____ be returning to work in no time at all.

Exercise 10
Complete the idiom phrase in each sentence.

1. He ached from head to _____ when he fell off the ladder.

2. If you call me _____ before noon, I'll still be at home.

3. After working in the fields all day, they were completely wiped

_____ .

4. She was burning _____ , so we applied a cold, wet washcloth.

5. He was running a _____ , but now he feels much better.

6. We were _____ on _____ feet after only two days of not feeling well.

7. They both came _____ with a sore throat.

8. Being worn _____ from bicycling, she lay down and rested.

9. In _____ time _____ all, we'll see each other again.

10. What's the _____ with the car? It won't start.

11. Whenever he _____ a cold, he doesn't go to work.

12. Just take it _____ ! Relax and don't worry.

Exercise 11
With a partner, create and perform an interesting, funny, enjoyable dialogue. Use as many idioms from this lesson as possible.

Exercise 12
Write sentences with the idioms given.

1. to come down with

_____

2. to call up (write the sentence in two ways)

_____

_____

3. to catch (an illness)

_____

4. from head to toe

_____

5. in no time at all

_____

6. worn out

_____

7. to take it easy

_____

8. to run a temperature

_____

Exercise 13
Circle the letter of the sentence that corresponds to the idiom used in the numbered sentence.

1. What's the matter with the television?
   a. Why are you purchasing a new television?
   b. Why aren't you watching television?
   c. Why isn't the television operating properly?
2. They love to take it easy on the California beaches.
   a. They love to lie in the sun.
   b. They love to swim all day.
   c. They love to run along the shore.
3. The doctor told us that visitors frequently come down with the disease.
   a. Visitors develop resistance to the disease.
   b. Visitors get the disease.
   c. Visitors are immune to the disease.

4. He feels worn out after mountain climbing.

   a. He feels good.

   b. He feels full of energy.

   c. He feels dizzy and weak.

5. She catches a cold when she's exposed to changes in temperature.

   a. Her body becomes cold.

   b. She begins to sneeze.

   c. She enjoys perfect health.

6. The hot sun made them feel as if they were running a temperature.

   a. The hot sun made them feel good.

   b. The hot sun made them want to run.

   c. The hot sun made them feel feverish.

7. Their relationship is back on its feet again.

   a. It is at a standstill.

   b. It is becoming worse.

   c. It is improving.

8. We will be there in no time at all.

   a. We will arrive shortly.

   b. We will arrive eventually.

   c. We will arrive later.

9. Whenever he overexercises, he feels like he's burning up.

   a. He continues exercising.

   b. He feels feverish.

   c. He feels good.

10. The clown was covered with paint from head to toe.

    a. Only his head was covered with paint.

    b. Only his toe was covered with paint.

    c. His entire body was covered with paint.

11. She was wiped out emotionally after the ordeal.

    a. She was full of energy and vigor.

    b. She knew what the problem was.

    c. She had no desire to do anything.

12. They call each other up weekly.

    a. They visit each other.

    b. They go out together.

    c. They telephone each other.

Exercise 14

Use the proper auxiliary verb after *but* and *and*. Use *either* or *too* as needed.

Example: He *likes* to swim, *but* she *doesn't*.
(affirmative, negative)
She *doesn't* like to swim, *but* he *does*.
(negative, affirmative)

Example: He *likes* to swim, *and* she *does too*.
(affirmative, affirmative)
He *doesn't* like to swim, *and* she *doesn't either*.
(negative, negative)

1. I prefer juice, and he _____ _____ .

2. They don't like steak, and we _____ _____ .

3. We want to leave early, but they _____ .

4. You are doing well, and they _____ _____ .

5. He has a dog, but his friend _____ .

6. I'll be there, but she _____ .

7. She would like a cup of coffee, and I _____ _____ .

8. They won't go by plane, but we _____ .

9. I saw that movie, but he _____ .

10. We don't plan on driving to New York, and they _____

_____ .

11. She has many friends, and he _____ _____ .

12. I would like to plant more flowers, and they _____

_____ .

13. He passed the test with flying colors, but she _____ .

14. They don't like the northern winters, but their friends _____ .

15. They enjoy living in the United States, and their families _____

_____ .

Heading up to the Mountains

Ana: I'm **looking forward** to the long weekend, David. It's been such a hectic week! We've been running here, running there, always **on the go**.

David: Well, Ana. I don't think we need **to think twice** about how we'd like to spend our **time off**.

Ana: That's for sure. After **taking care of** a few **odds and ends,** let's **head up to** the mountains and take it easy . . .

David: Away from the **rat race** of city life!

Ana: **You said it!** When we're off in the mountains, we can unwind and **take our minds off** all the daily hassles.

David: And we can do whatever we **feel like** doing—hiking, fishing, swimming, or just listening to the relaxing world around us.

Ana: Let's not waste our time talking about it, David. Let's **get the show on the road!**

Definitions

to look forward to: to be enthusiastic about, to eagerly anticipate, to expect

She is looking forward to the movie. She expects to enjoy it.

on the go: very busy, continuously doing something, going somewhere

They're always on the go. They're always doing something.

to think twice: to reconsider, to think carefully

We had to think twice about getting a new car. We had to think very carefully about it.

time off: time without work, free time

We enjoy our time off from work. We enjoy our free time when we aren't working.

to take care of: to attend to, to observe, to deal with

We have to take care of our car. We have to attend to it (repair it).

odds and ends: small items of relative unimportance, various things

They only need a few odds and ends to finish decorating the house. They only need a few more small things.

to head up to (to head down to): to go toward, to go in the direction of

We head up to the mountains every weekend. We go to the mountains every weekend.

rat race: a confusing rush, a confusing struggle

Their life was a rat race. Their life was a confusing struggle.

You said it!: to show strong agreement with another person

You said it! We need a new library! I strongly agree with you; we need a new library!

to take one's mind off: to stop thinking about, to forget, not to think about

It took my mind off the problem. It made me forget the problem.

to feel like: to want to, to have the desire to

They feel like going to an early movie. They want to go to an early movie.

to get the show on the road: to prepare everything and leave

Let's get the show on the road, guys! Let's get everything ready and leave!

None of these idioms may be separated by the object.

Exercise 1
Answer these questions from the dialogue orally.

1. What is Ana looking forward to?

166

2. How have David and Ana been on the go?

3. Why don't they have to think twice about how they'd like to spend their time off?

4. Where are they heading up to after taking care of a few odds and ends?

5. What do David and Ana want to get away from?

6. Why does Ana say, "You said it!"?

7. How does being in the mountains help them unwind and take their minds off the daily hassles?

8. What might they feel like doing?

9. What does Ana mean when she says, "Let's get the show on the road!"?

Exercise 2
Write the idioms from the dialogue that correspond to the words in parentheses.

1. Ana is (anticipating) _____ the long weekend.

2. David and Ana are always (very busy) _____ .

3. They don't need (to think carefully) _____ about what they want to do.

4. Ana and David know how they want to spend their (free time) _____

_____ .

5. After (attending to) _____ various things, they'll be going to the mountains.

6. After attending to (various things) _____ , they'll be going to the mountains.

7. After attending to various things, they (go to) _____ the mountains.

8. Ana and David don't like the (confusing rush) _____ of city life.

9. "(I agree with you) _____ !" Ana said.

10. They need to (stop thinking about) _____

    _____ the daily hassles.

11. They can do whatever they (want to) _____
    doing.

12. Let's (prepare everything quickly and leave) _____

    _____ .

Exercise 3
Answer these questions orally.

1. Do you have to think twice about where to head to (head up to) when you have time off?
2. Do you look forward to unwinding and taking your mind off everyday problems?
3. What do you often feel like doing?
4. Are there many odds and ends you have to take care of before getting the show on the road?
5. Are you the kind of person who is usually on the go and in the rat race?
6. When might you say, "You said it!", when you're talking about time off?

Exercise 4
Match the idiom to its definition by writing the letter of the definition on the line next to the idiom number.

1. _____ odds and ends   a. free time

2. _____ to think twice   b. to show strong agreement

3. _____ to look forward to   c. various things

4. _____ to head up to   d. to prepare everything and leave

5. _____ on the go   e. to reconsider

6. _____ time off   f. a confusing struggle

7. _____ to take care of

8. _____ to get the show on the road

9. _____ You said it!

10. _____ to feel like

11. _____ rat race

12. _____ to take one's mind off

g. to anticipate eagerly

h. very busy

i. to attend to

j. to go toward

k. to forget

l. to want to

Exercise 5
Respond to these statements orally.

1. Name two movies you look forward to seeing.
2. Name one type of recreation that helps you take your mind off problems.
3. Name two places you feel like visiting.
4. Name one mountain you've headed up to.
5. Name some things you do when you have time off.
6. Name three odds and ends you have to take care of.

Exercise 6
Underline the words in parentheses that best correspond to the italicized idioms.

1. We are *looking forward to* visiting them. We are (reconsidering, enthusiastic about, uneasy about) visiting them.
2. They enjoy *time off* from work. They enjoy (not having to work, not having a vacation, working every day).
3. They need to buy some *odds and ends* before leaving on their trip. They need to buy (flight tickets, suitcases, deodorant and toothpaste).
4. He *headed up to* his friend's house last week. He (went to, didn't go to, failed to go to) his friend's house last week.
5. I love a night of enjoyment after a day *on the go*. I love a night of enjoyment after a (very busy, lazy, relaxing) day.
6. We *took care of* some odds and ends before leaving. We (completed, forgot to do, anticipated) them.

169

7. He had *to think twice* about spending so much money. He had to (forget, think carefully, be confused) about it.

8. Her life became a *rat race*. Her life became (relaxed, easy, a confusing rush).

9. I *feel like* going to a Spanish restaurant. I (don't want to, have no desire to, want to) go to a Spanish restaurant.

10. When he goes out, he *takes his mind off* the things that bother him. When he goes out, he (discusses, thinks about, doesn't think about) the things that bother him.

11. Let's *get the show on the road*. Let's (stay home, go to a show, get going).

12. *You said it!* This is a terrible dinner! (I agree with you, I don't agree with you, You can't be right) about the dinner!

Exercise 7
Reread the dialogue. Tell the story in your own words using the idioms.

Exercise 8
Complete the second sentence by substituting idioms for the italicized words.

1. We have *various things* to take care of.

   We have _____ to take care of.

2. They enjoy being *very busy.*

   They enjoy being _____ .

3. Let's *prepare everything and leave.*

   Let's _____ .

4. Dancing is a pleasant way to spend *free time.*

   Dancing is a pleasant way to spend _____ .

5. We try *to attend to* everything we have to do.

   We try _____ everything we have to do.

6. It was a *confusing rush* while living in the city.

   It was a _____ while living in the city.

7. How do you *stop thinking about* those things?

   How do you _____ those things?

8. He's *eagerly anticipating* the date with her.

   He's _____ the date with her.

9. Do you have *to think carefully* about how you want to spend your vacation?

   Do you have _____ about how you want to spend your vacation?

10. We're *going to* the Lakes Region tomorrow.

    We're _____ the Lakes Region tomorrow.

11. *I agree with you!* This summer is unbelievably hot!

    _____ ! This summer is unbelievably hot!

12. What do you *want* to do?

    What do you _____ doing?

Exercise 9
Change these sentences by inserting the proper word in parentheses.

Example: He started the car up.

        He started the car up ___*easily*___ . (easy, easily)

1. We've been wanting to head up to the mountains.

   We've been wanting to head up to the mountains _____

   _____ a long time. (since, for)

171

2. She's part of the rat race!

She's _____ part of the rat race! (certain, certainly)

3. We're looking forward to seeing them.

We're looking forward to seeing them _____ . (very much, very many)

4. You need time off.

You _____ need time off. (definite, definitely)

5. We have odds and ends to do everyday.

We have _____ odds and ends to do everyday. (much, many)

6. Take care of our money!

Take care of our _____ money! (hard-earned, hardly earned)

7. She never thinks twice before making a decision.

She never thinks twice before making _____ decision. (any, no)

8. You said it! Having a long vacation is terrific!

You said it! Having a long vacation is _____ terrific! (real, really)

9. They are on the go because they are trying to get ahead.

They are on the go because they are trying _____ to get ahead. (hard, hardly)

10. Ana takes her mind off her work by reading a book.

Ana takes her mind off her work by reading a _____ book. (good, best)

11. We need to pack up and get the show on the road.

   We need to pack up _____ and get the show
   on the road. (quick, quickly)

12. Do you feel like walking through the park?

   Do you feel like walking _____ through the
   park? (slow, slowly)

Exercise 10
Complete the idiom phrase in each sentence.

1. We need to think _____ about this trip. It's going to be
   more expensive than we had anticipated.

2. I have some odds and _____ to take care of. I have to go
   to the bank, the post office, and the pharmacy.

3. Let's head _____ _____ the mountains. It will be
   quiet and peaceful there.

4. You're always on _____ _____ . When do you
   have time to relax?

5. If we get the _____ on the _____ early, there
   won't be so much traffic.

6. You _____ it! It's been raining too much!

7. She can't take her _____ _____ him. She thinks
   about him all the time.

8. Forget the rat _____ ! Stop rushing so much, and take it
   easy!

9. What do you feel _____ eating? We can have fish, steak,
   pizza, sushi, falafel, or whatever else you might want.

10. He's looking _____ to seeing his friend again. He hasn't
    seen him for many months.

11. When we have time _____ , we'll finish fixing up the apartment.

12. Please take _____ of our cat while we're gone. Be sure she has enough food and water.

Exercise 11
With a partner, create and perform an interesting, funny, enjoyable dialogue. Use as many idioms from this lesson as possible.

Exercise 12
Write sentences with the idioms given.

1. rat race

    _____

2. odds and ends

    _____

3. to take one's mind off

    _____

4. to feel like

    _____

5. to look forward to

    _____

6. to take care of

    _____

7. time off

    _____

8. on the go

_____

Exercise 13
Circle the letter of the sentence that corresponds to the idiom used in the numbered sentence.

1. Think twice about giving him any more money.

   a. Reconsider giving him any more money.

   b. Don't give him any more money.

   c. It's impossible to give him any more money.

2. She loved the rat race of her new job.

   a. She had plenty of free time.

   b. She didn't have much to do.

   c. She was constantly on the go.

3. He totally enjoyed having time off.

   a. He totally enjoyed going to work.

   b. He totally enjoyed being able to do whatever he felt like doing.

   c. He totally enjoyed his job.

4. You said it! We really got our money's worth.

   a. I agree that we got our money's worth.

   b. I don't know if we got our money's worth.

   c. Did you say we got our money's worth?

5. They found many odds and ends when they were cleaning the closets.

   a. They found the video camera.

   b. They found broken crayons.

   c. They found a gold necklace.

6. She's always on the go, and she loves it.

   a. She's lazy.

   b. She never does anything.

   c. She's energetic.

7. They're heading up to visit their relatives.

   a. Their relatives live in the North.

   b. Their relatives live in the South.

   c. Their relatives live in the Midwest.

8. The newcomers were looking forward to living in the city.

   a. They were depressed about living in the city.

   b. They were excited about living in the city.

   c. They didn't want to live in the city.

9. He feels like leaving his job.

   a. He feels good about his job.

   b. He wants to keep his job.

   c. He doesn't want to keep his job.

10. He was so infatuated with her that he couldn't take his mind off her.

   a. He rarely thought about her.

   b. He thought about her constantly.

   c. He forgot about her.

11. They took care of the house while their friends were away.

   a. They took things from the house.

   b. They left the doors and windows unlocked.

   c. They checked the house daily.

12. We have to get the show on the road by 7:00 a.m.

   a. We have to start getting ready by 7:00 a.m.

   b. We have to leave by 7:00 a.m.

   c. We have to be awake by 7:00 a.m.

Exercise 14

Supply the appropriate preposition in each sentence. Use *without, of, on, over, up, out, in, into, to.*

1. Where can we sign _____ for courses at the college?

2. He put _____ many hours of studying before taking the exam.

3. I picked _____ these flowers at the Floral Shop.

4. Pick _____ the one you want. You have a choice of two colors.

5. She started _____ the car and left.

6. They plan _____ being here by noon.

7. She did _____ the bedroom, and it looks beautiful!

8. There's an excellent sale going _____ at the mall.

9. My appliances are quite old and always acting _____ .

10. You need to write _____ a check for $150.

11. You can do _____ a dishwasher if you have to.

12. Let's eat _____ tonight.

13. I was about _____ leave when the phone rang.

14. Are you going to put more money _____ this car?

15. It's probably better to trade it _____ .

16. Call me _____ before you leave.

17. He's totally worn _____ from all this work.

18. Take care _____ him when I leave.

19. It kept _____ snowing all night.

20. Think it _____ , and we'll discuss it tomorrow.

Lesson 13

Keeping in Touch

David: What's the matter with Kim, Ana? It sounds like you had an urgent phone call from her this morning.

Ana: I don't know exactly. We had planned on *getting together* this weekend to figure out our vacation, but she had to suddenly *put everything off*. Something very important had *come up*.

David: I'm sorry to hear that. It's not like Kim *to break an engagement*.

Ana: Well, her mother's been ill, and Kim's been having trouble *keeping in touch* with her. They had been *taking turns dropping each other a line every other* week, but now it's been *ages* since Kim's heard from her.

David: Well, aren't the letters *getting through?*

Ana: Not always. The mail in and out of her native country is often delayed or lost.

David: Maybe you should *give Kim a ring later on* and see if everything is all right.

Ana: I plan to, David. Maybe I can be of help to her.

Definitions

to get together: to meet or visit with each other, to see and talk with each other

We got together at his house. We met at his house.

to put off: to postpone, to delay, to do later

Why did they put their meeting off? Why did they postpone it?

to come up: to emerge unexpectedly, to occur, to arise

When did the problem come up? When did the problem emerge?

to break an (the) engagement: to cancel an appointment, meeting, or date

She broke the engagement because she was ill. She cancelled the meeting because she was ill.

to keep in touch: to maintain contact, to continue to communicate

Ana and Kim keep in touch. They maintain contact with each other.

to take turns: to alternate, to do one after the other

They took turns calling each other up. They alternated in their phone calls to each other.

to drop (someone) a line: to write a short letter or note

Please drop me a line soon. Please write me a short letter.

every other: every second, every alternate, alternating

They meet every other weekend. They meet every second weekend.

ages: a (very) long time

I haven't seen him for ages! I haven't seen him for a very long time!

to get through: to make a connection, to go toward a destination, to pass through

Although we called many times, we couldn't get through. Although we called many times, we couldn't make a phone connection.

to give someone a ring: to telephone, to call on the telephone

He gave us a ring from the airport. He called us from the airport.

later on: not now, later

I'll be there later on. I'll be there later.

The following idiom may be separated by the object. This idiom may be said in two ways:

to put off:

> We put off the meeting.
> We put the meeting off.

Exercise 1
Answer these questions from the dialogue orally.

1. Why had Ana and Kim planned on getting together?
2. Why did Kim have to suddenly put everything off?
3. What had come up?
4. Does Kim usually break engagements?
5. Why has Kim been having trouble keeping in touch with her mother?
6. How have they been taking turns dropping each other a line?
7. How often is every other week?
8. What does Ana mean that it's been ages since Kim's heard from her mother?
9. Are the letters between Kim and her mother getting through?
10. Why should Ana give Kim a ring later on?

Exercise 2
Write the idioms from the dialogue that correspond to the words in parentheses.

1. Ana and Kim had planned on (meeting with each other) _____

   _____ .

2. Kim had to (postpone) _____ everything _____ .

3. Something important had (arisen) _____ .

4. It's not like Kim (to cancel a meeting) _____

   _____ .

5. Kim and her mother have been having trouble (maintaining contact)

   _____ .

181

6. They had been (alternating) _____
   maintaining contact.

7. They had been alternating (writing) _____

   each other _____ .

8. They wrote (every second) _____ week.

9. It's been (a long time) _____ since Kim's
   heard from her mother.

10. Isn't the mail (making a connection) _____ ?

11. Ana will (telephone) _____ Kim _____

    _____ .

12. She will telephone her (later) _____ .

Exercise 3
Answer these questions orally.

1. Do you keep in touch with faraway relatives by dropping them a line
   or by giving them a ring?
2. Have you ever had trouble getting through to them?
3. When you get together with friends, do you take turns deciding what
   to do?
4. Do any of your friends frequently break or put off an engagement
   with you?
5. When was the last time something unexpected came up when you had
   a date with a friend?
6. How often do you go out if you go out every other night?
7. How often do you go out if you haven't gone out for ages?
8. Where do you plan to go later on today?

Exercise 4
Match the idiom to its definition by writing the letter of the definition on the line next to the idiom number.

1. _____ to give someone a ring   a. to meet with each other

2. _____ later on   b. to emerge unexpectedly

3. _____ to put off   c. to telephone

4. _____ to come up   d. to maintain contact

5. _____ to get through   e. to cancel a date

6. _____ every other   f. later

7. _____ to drop someone a line   g. to make a connection

8. _____ to break an
engagement   h. every second

   i. to postpone

9. _____ ages

   j. a very long time

10. _____ to take turns

   k. to write a short letter

11. _____ to keep in touch

   l. to alternate

12. _____ to get together

Exercise 5
Respond to these statements orally.

1. Give three ways to keep in touch.
2. Give two reasons for dropping someone a line.
3. Give one reason for breaking an engagement.
4. Name two things you like to do every other weekend.
5. Name one time a letter of yours didn't get through.
6. Name two people you want to get together with.
7. Name one occurrence that caused you to put off a visit.

Exercise 6
Underline the words in parentheses that best correspond to the italicized idioms.

1. She will *drop him a line.* She will (call him, write him a short letter, visit him).

2. I must call up the girls *later on.* I must call up the girls (now, later, within five minutes).

3. They *put off* the meeting. They (didn't delay, forgot about, postponed) the meeting.

4. We *get together* whenever we can. We (write each other a letter, meet each other, call each other up).

5. He has to cancel his appointment because something *came up.* Something (might occur, will occur, occurred).

6. They like to *keep in touch.* They like to (maintain contact, avoid contact, have nothing to do with each other).

7. I'll *give you a ring* tonight. I'll (visit you, call you, write you).

8. The letter *got through* easily. The letter (got lost, reached its destination, was never sent).

9. I haven't seen them for *ages.* I haven't seen them (since yesterday, for a long time, for two weeks).

10. We used to go to the movies *every other* Saturday. We used to go to the movies (alternating Saturdays, every Saturday, once on Saturday).

11. Kim and Ana *take turns* writing letters. (Only Kim, Only Ana, First one then the other) writes letters.

12. He *broke their engagement* two weeks in advance. He (ignored, cancelled, forgot) their engagement.

Exericse 7
Reread the dialogue. Tell the story in your own words using the idioms.

Exercise 8
Complete the second sentence by substituting idioms for the italicized words.

1. They *write a short letter* to their sister very often.

   They _____ to their sister very often.

2. David has been trying *to make a connection* with his friend.

   David has been trying _____ to his friend.

3. She visited Kim *a very long time* ago.

   She visited Kim _____ ago.

4. Let's *continue to communicate.*

   Let's _____ .

5. I'll call you up *alternating* Sundays.

   I'll call you up _____ Sunday.

6. We can go on vacation *later.*

   We can go on vacation _____ .

7. She *telephoned* me last night.

   She _____ me _____
   last night.

8. Why did you *cancel the date* with her?

   Why did you _____ with her?

9. They will *meet each other* at the park.

   They will _____ at the park.

10. Something very important *emerged unexpectedly.*

    Something very important _____ .

11. They *delayed* the meeting until next week.

    They _____ the meeting until next week.

12. Sometimes, they *alternate* telephoning each other.

    Sometimes, they _____ telephoning
    each other.

Exercise 9

Change these sentences to the past tense.

Example: The car *continues* to act up.

The car ____*Continued*____ to act up.

1. We *will find* out the answer later on.

   We _____ out the answer later on.

2. They *will break* their dinner engagement.

   They _____ their dinner engagement.

3. They *get* together when the weather *is* nice.

   They _____ together when the weather

   _____ nice.

4. The mail *gets* through, but it *is* very slow.

   The mail _____ through, but it _____

   _____ very slow.

5. When something *comes* up, he *calls* her immediately.

   When something _____ up, he _____

   _____ her immediately.

6. The rendezvous *will be* every other weekend.

   The rendezvous _____ every other weekend.

7. They *keep* in touch by dropping each other a line.

   They _____ in touch by dropping each other
   a line.

8. Sometimes I *don't* call him up for ages.

   Sometimes I _____ call him up for ages.

9. *Do* they usually take turns driving?

_____ they usually take turns driving?

10. She *puts* off writing letters when she *can*.

She _____ off writing letters when she

_____ .

11. He *gives* her a ring from the office.

He _____ her a ring from the office.

12. I *will drop* you a line from San Francisco.

I _____ you a line from San Francisco.

Exercise 10
Complete the idiom phrase in each sentence.

1. I will meet you later _____ ; now I am too busy.

2. He received a paycheck every _____ week, but it never lasted more than seven days.

3. Let's keep _____ _____ as often as possible. I'll want to know how you are doing.

4. I'll drop you a _____ as soon as I arrive in Switzerland.

5. She broke the _____ with her friend because she didn't feel well.

6. Let's get _____ this afternoon. I have something to discuss with you.

7. Something came _____ very suddenly, and she immediately left the party.

8. If you put _____ what you have to do today, you'll still have to do it tomorrow.

9. It's been _____ since we last saw them, perhaps eight years.

10. If we take _____ driving, neither one of us will get too tired.

11. We couldn't get _____ to them by telephone, so we wrote a letter.

12. I'll give you a _____ at 11:00 p.m. Please be there to receive the call.

Exercise 11
With a partner, create and perform an interesting, funny, enjoyable dialogue. Use as many idioms from this lesson as possible.

Exercise 12
Write sentences with the idioms given.

1. to take turns

_____

2. every other

_____

3. to come up

_____

4. to get together

_____

5. to get through

_____

6. to keep in touch

_____

7. to put off (write the sentence in two ways)

_____

_____

8. to give someone a ring

_____

Exercise 13
Circle the letter of the sentence that corresponds to the idiom used in the numbered sentence.

1. The new job requires her to work every other day.

   a. She has to work Tuesday, Thursday, and Saturday.

   b. She has to work Monday, Tuesday, and Thursday.

   c. She has to work Tuesday, Wednesday, and Thursday.

2. He hadn't seen his brother for ages.

   a. He hadn't seen him for a few weeks.

   b. He hadn't seen him since they were teenagers.

   c. He hadn't seen him for a few days.

3. We can go swimming later on, but now let's finish our work.

   a. We can go swimming in a few minutes.

   b. We can't go swimming at all because we need to finish our work.

   c. We can go swimming in a few hours.

4. The governor keeps in touch with the people.

   a. He ignores them.

   b. He communicates with them.

   c. He has no contact with them.

5. They couldn't get through the street because it was being paved.

   a. They couldn't drive on that street.

   b. They could drive on the shoulder of the street.

   c. They could drive on the street if they were careful.

6. The librarian gave her a ring to return the books.

   a. The librarian telephoned her.

   b. The librarian wrote her a note.

   c. The librarian visited her.

7. Drop me a line when the work is completed.

    a. Call me.

    b. Visit me.

    c. Write to me.

8. When he broke the engagement, his boss became angry.

    a. His boss became angry when he didn't attend the meeting.

    b. His boss became angry when he arrived late.

    c. His boss became angry when he broke the computer terminal.

9. They took turns driving to work.

    a. They never drove to work.

    b. They alternated driving to work.

    c. The same person always drove to work.

10. When problem after problem came up, they decided against buying the house.

    a. Problems failed to emerge.

    b. Problems continued to emerge.

    c. Problems were resolved immediately.

11. He put off attending college because he didn't have the money.

    a. He didn't attend college immediately.

    b. He attended college immediately.

    c. He insisted on attending college immediately.

12. Getting together is sheer joy!

    a. Being with each other is sheer joy!

    b. Writing each other is sheer joy!

    c. Talking on the phone is sheer joy!

Exercise 14

Use either *for* or *since* in the following sentences.

Example: I naven't seen him *since* Tuesday.
        (*since* is used with a *specific* time)
        I haven't seen him *for* two days.
        (*for* is used with a *duration* of time)

1. We haven't had a vacation _____ a long time.

   We haven't had a vacation _____ last year.

2. They have been students _____ January.

   They have been students _____ five months.

3. I have been working there _____ one year.

   I have been working there _____ June 1990.

4. He's been driving back and forth to work _____ eight weeks.

   He's been driving back and forth to work _____ April.

5. She's had her driver's license _____ many years.

   She's had her driver's license _____ she was sixteen.

6. We have been using this book _____ September.

   We have been using this book _____ six months.

7. They have been married _____ last month.

   They have been married _____ one month.

8. He's been going by subway _____ he first came to the city.

   He's been going by subway _____ two years.

9. We've been waiting _____ 9:45.

   We've been waiting _____ one hour.

10. We've been living here _____ two years now.

    We've been living here _____ we bought this house.

Mapping out a Vacation

David: Let's **map out** our vacation to Washington, D.C., Ana.

Ana: Good idea. I'm looking forward to seeing the capital of the United States and the White House. So many people **rave about** it.

David: It should be very enjoyable now that we have time off and enough money **put aside** for the trip, **spending money,** and an emergency if something should **go wrong.**

Ana: You know, David. I would really prefer to travel by air, but I know you're right. We'll be **better off** going by car.

David: It'll be less expensive, and we can **make good time** if we get going early in the day. We can be **on the road** before dawn and put some good hours of travel in.

Ana: That's true. And in the evening we can **pull in** at any one of the many motels along the way and **check in** for the night.

David: Exactly. Then when we get to Washington, D.C., we can pick up numerous brochures and see what we feel like doing.

Ana: I'm definitely counting on stopping in at the House of Representatives and seeing government officials.

David: Well, Ana, we even **stand a chance** of **shaking hands** with the president.

Ana: That would be a truly memorable occasion, wouldn't it?

David: It certainly would be! And it would make this a top-notch vacation.

Definitions

to map out: to plan, to organize, to schedule

They mapped out the itinerary of their trip. They planned their itinerary.

to rave about: to be extremely enthusiastic or excited about, to praise greatly

He absolutely raved about the movie! He praised it tremendously!

spending money: extra money to be used in any way one wants, extra money to be used for oneself

Did she give the children spending money? Did she give them money to be used for themselves?

to go wrong: to change from good to bad, to have misfortunes occur, to fail to occur as expected

Nothing went wrong during the trip. Nothing bad happened during the trip.

better off: in an improved situation or environment, in more advantageous circumstances, more fortunate

They are better off living in the country. They are more fortunate living there.

to make good time: to cover a distance quickly, to progress rapidly, to travel or go fast

They made good time traveling on the expressway. They traveled quickly.

to put aside: to save

He put aside $500 for the trip. He saved $500 for the trip.

on the road: traveling, going somewhere

How long was she on the road? How long was she traveling?

to pull in: to stop (at), to arrive

We pulled in at a motel. We stopped at a motel.

to check in: to register at lodging quarters, to register at specific meetings, to sign one's name on a list

   Did they check in at the hotel yet? Did they register at the hotel yet?

to stand a chance: to have a possibility, might

   We stand a chance of meeting them here. We have a possibility of meeting them here.

to shake hands: to clasp right hands in greeting or parting

   We shook hands when we met. We clasped right hands.

The following idioms may be separated by the object. These idioms may be said in two ways.

to map out:

   He is mapping out the route.
   He is mapping the route out.

to put aside:

   They put aside plenty of money.
   They put plenty of money aside.

Exercise 1
Answer these questions from the dialogue orally.

1. What are David and Ana mapping out?
2. What do people rave about?
3. For what have they put money aside?
4. Why do David and Ana need spending money?
5. How have they prepared for something going wrong?
6. Why will they be better off going by car?
7. How can David and Ana make good time?
8. How many hours of travel can they put in if they are on the road before dawn?
9. Where can David and Ana pull in for the night?
10. How does a person check in at a motel?
11. Do David and Ana stand a chance of shaking hands with the president? Why?

Exercise 2

Write the idioms from the dialogue that correspond to the words in parentheses.

1. David and Ana are (planning) _____ their vacation.

2. Many people (greatly praise) _____ the capital.

3. David and Ana have (saved) _____ money for the trip.

4. They have enough (extra money to be used for whatever they want)

   _____ .

5. They also have money for an emergency if something should (occur

   that is bad) _____ .

6. Ana agrees that they will be (in more advantageous circumstances)

   _____ going by car.

7. They can (cover a distance quickly) _____ if they leave early.

8. David and Ana can be (traveling) _____ by dawn.

9. In the evening, they can (stop) _____ at one of the motels.

10. They can (register) _____ for the night.

11. David and Ana (have a possibility) _____ of seeing the president.

12. They might even (clasp right hands) _____ with him.

Exercise 3

Answer these questions orally.

1. What vacation place have you heard people rave about?
2. Do you stand a chance of going there this year?
3. In what way does it help you to map out your itinerary in advance?
4. How much money would you need to put aside for the trip?
5. How much spending money do you usually need?
6. What could go wrong on a trip?
7. How are you better off traveling, by air or by car?
8. Do you make good time traveling by car? Explain.
9. What kinds of things can you do while you're on the road?
10. Which restaurants do you pull in at when you're hungry?
11. Where do you check in for the night?
12. Is there anyone special you would like to shake hands with while on vacation?

Exercise 4

Match the idiom to its definition by writing the letter of the definition on the line next to the idiom number.

1. _____ to make good time

2. _____ to put aside

3. _____ on the road

4. _____ to stand a chance

5. _____ to shake hands

6. _____ to map out

7. _____ better off

8. _____ to go wrong

9. _____ to rave about

10. _____ to check in

a. extra money to be used for oneself

b. to stop (at)

c. to have a possibility

d. to fail to occur as expected

e. to praise greatly

f. to plan

g. to register

h. to clasp right hands

i. traveling

j. to save

11. _____ to pull in   k. to travel fast

12. _____ spending money   l. in an improved situation

Exercise 5
Respond to these statements orally.

1. Name one way to make good time while traveling.
2. Name one hotel that you rave about.
3. Name two people you would like to shake hands with.
4. Name two things that can go wrong on a trip.
5. Give one reason for not spending a long day on the road.
6. Give one reason for needing spending money.
7. Give two reasons for mapping out a trip in advance of leaving.

Exercise 6
Underline the words in parentheses that best correspond to the italicized idioms.

1. They have a lot of *spending money*. They have a lot of money for (themselves, monthly bills, emergencies).
2. The children are *better off* in this school. They are (in a worse environment, in an improved environment, in the same environment).
3. He wondered what could *go wrong*. He wondered what (bad things might occur, good things would occur, could be better).
4. She *raved about* the view from her hotel room. She (was angry about, complained about, was excited about) the view.
5. We *mapped out* our journey across the United States. We (didn't plan, planned, had no plans for) our journey.
6. He *stands a chance* of winning the prize. He (might, definitely will, definitely won't) win the prize.
7. Do you *shake hands* when you meet your friends? Do you (wave to them, clasp right hands in greeting, point at them)?
8. They *checked in* at a beautiful hotel. They (signed their names, didn't register, wrote a check) at the hotel.
9. She *pulled in* as he was leaving. She (left, arrived, departed) as he was leaving.
10. They were *on the road* for many hours. They were (planning their trip, preparing to leave, traveling).

11. He *put aside* a lot of money. He (spent, borrowed, saved) a lot of money.

12. They *made good time* traveling at night. They (traveled quickly, traveled slowly, didn't travel) at night.

Exercise 7
Reread the dialogue. Tell the story in your own words using the idioms.

Exercise 8
Complete the second sentence by substituting idioms for the italicized words.

1. How did you *organize* your vacation?

   How did you _____ your vacation?

2. They are *more fortunate* now than they were before.

   They are _____ now than they were before.

3. We *traveled fast* during the night.

   We _____ during the night.

4. When we are introduced to someone, we *clasp right hands*.

   When we are introduced to someone, we _____ .

5. She *has a possibility* of having a vacation this month.

   She _____ of having a vacation this month.

6. They *saved* enough money for a three-week vacation.

   They _____ enough money for a three-week vacation.

7. Her parents gave her *extra money to be used for herself.*

   Her parents gave her _____ .

8. Which movie did she *greatly praise?*

   Which movie did she _____ ?

9. Nothing *bad occurred* during the trip.

   Nothing _____ during the trip.

10. We must *register* at the hotel early in the day.

    We must _____ at the hotel early in the day.

11. She's happiest when she is *going somewhere*.

    She's happiest when she is _____ .

12. Let's *stop* at the next restaurant.

    Let's _____ at the next restaurant.

Exercise 9
Change these sentences to the tense indicated by the word(s) in parentheses.

Example: We *kept* in touch with our friends.

   (everyday) We _____*keep*_____ in touch with our friends.

1. He *raves* about the movies.

   (now) He _____ about the movies.

2. They *were* better off than most people in the same situation.

   (in a few months) They _____ better off than most people in the same situation.

3. I *mapped* out my itinerary for the business trip.

   (later) I _____ out my itinerary for the business trip.

4. She *gives* me spending money.

   (yesterday) She _____ me spending money.

5. We *will pull* in at a hotel after we *have* our dinner.

(last night) We _____ in at a hotel after we

_____ our dinner.

6. We *will* check in at the new hotel.

(on our previous visit) We _____ in at the
new hotel.

7. They *shook* hands when they *met*.

(always) They _____ hands when they

_____ .

8. He *made* good time because he *was traveling* on the expressway.

(now) He _____ good time because he

_____ on the expressway.

9. She *stands* a chance of seeing him.

(yesterday) She _____ a chance of seeing
him.

10. She *put* aside $50 for souvenirs.

(tomorrow) She _____ aside $50 for
souvenirs.

11. Something *might go* wrong with the thermostat.

(this past weekend) Something _____ wrong
with the thermostat.

12. We *were* on the road by dawn.

(tomorrow) We _____ on the road by dawn.

Exercise 10
Complete the idiom phrase in each sentence.

1. If we map _____ our vacation carefully, we'll know exactly which routes we want to take.

2. It seemed like everything went _____ ! There was a big hurricane, the hotel lost our reservations, and someone stole our car!

3. Next time we'll be better _____ going by plane. We wasted a lot of time by driving.

4. We can make _____ time by traveling at night. There won't be much traffic, so we'll be able to travel more quickly.

5. They put _____ one week's salary. They saved it for new tires.

6. She loves being _____ the road. She loves traveling and seeing new places.

7. They checked _____ at a very expensive hotel. They paid $200 a night.

8. The child was very excited about _____ hands with the president. It was an occasion he would always remember.

9. If you save all your money for the next two months, you _____ a chance of going to Europe this summer.

10. Everyone was raving _____ the Broadway show! They said it was the best one they had ever seen!

11. Her grandmother gave her _____ money for all the extra things she wanted to buy.

12. If we pull _____ at a motel by 6:00 p.m., we'll still have the evening to go out.

Exercise 11
With a partner, create and perform an interesting, funny, enjoyable dialogue. Use as many idioms from this lesson as possible.

Exercise 12
Write sentences with the idioms given.

1. to put aside (write the sentence in two ways)

   _____

   _____

2. to make good time

   _____

3. to stand a chance

   _____

4. to rave about

   _____

5. better off

   _____

6. to go wrong

   _____

7. on the road

   _____

8. to check in

   _____

Exercise 13
Circle the letter of the sentence that corresponds to the idiom used in the numbered sentence.

1. They shook hands with all the passersby.
   a. They nodded at the passersby.
   b. They clasped hands with the passersby.
   c. They waved to the passersby.

2. He pulled in at work thirty minutes late.

   a. He left work thirty minutes late.

   b. He took a break from work thirty minutes late.

   c. He arrived at work thirty minutes late.

3. We forgot to check in at the conference.

   a. We registered at the conference.

   b. We didn't register at the conference.

   c. We remembered to sign our names at the conference.

4. The airplane made good time because of a tail wind.

   a. The airplane lost its tail in the wind.

   b. The airplane flew fast because of the wind.

   c. The airplane flew slowly because of the wind.

5. They stand a chance of going to the Far East.

   a. They are definitely going to the Far East.

   b. They are definitely not going to the Far East.

   c. They might go to the Far East.

6. Everything seemed to go wrong at the same time.

   a. Everything was at a standstill.

   b. Everything improved.

   c. Everything deteriorated.

7. They mapped out the structure of the new city.

   a. They had no idea how the city would look.

   b. They knew how the city would look.

   c. They didn't know how the city would look.

8. He raved about her cooking.

   a. Her cooking was out of this world.

   b. Her cooking was terrible.

   c. Her cooking was mediocre.

9. The grandparents gave their grandchildren spending money.

   a. They gave them money for ice cream cones.

   b. They gave them money for family groceries.

   c. They gave them money for car repairs.

10. They were better off before the war than after the war.

    a. They had more food before the war.

    b. They had no food before the war.

    c. They had less food before the war.

11. They put aside their problems when visitors come.

    a. They discuss their problems with the visitors.

    b. They pretend they are happy.

    c. The visitors create problems.

12. A news reporter spends a lot of time on the road.

    a. A news reporter spends a lot of time in the office.

    b. A news reporter spends a lot of time at the TV station.

    c. A news reporter spends a lot of time going from one assignment to another.

Exercise 14

Supply the appropriate preposition in each sentence. Use *up, in, with, for, out of, off, at, of, down on, on.*

1. How much did you pay _____ that dress? It looks very expensive.

2. He is afraid _____ dogs and never goes near them.

3. Everyone laughed _____ Mike's funny joke. They really enjoyed it.

4. I got _____ the bus at Lexington Street because that's where my friend lives.

5. She had to get _____ early in the morning to catch the 6:00 a.m. flight.

6. We looked everywhere _____ the missing ring, but we couldn't find it.

7. They have to leave before the custodian locks the doors, or they won't be able to get _____ _____ the building.

8. He wakes _____ late every morning because he never sets his alarm clock.

9. If you don't know the meaning of the word, look it _____ in the dictionary.

10. We arrived _____ Chicago _____ the airport at midnight.

11. He got _____ his bicycle and rode away.

12. Don't tell me you went _____ him! I thought you don't like him.

13. He always looks _____   _____ everybody. He has a superiority complex.

14. It depends _____ the weather. If it's a beautiful weekend, we can head down to the shore.

15. _____ present, we are doing very well. We're getting used to everything around us.

Lesson 15

Settling Down

David: Well, Ana, I think we've finally **settled down!**

Ana: I think so, too, David. We don't feel like strangers in a new land anymore, do we?

David: No, we don't. Although we've had our share of being **hard up** and having trouble **making ends meet,** we always believed we could make it.

Ana: Well, **for the most part,** we were optimistic and determined to have our dreams **come true.**

David: And guess what—they are! Once we **snapped out of** our initial culture shock, we got used to the world around us and began taking advantage of it.

Ana: That's for sure. We got going with our education and really **zeroed in on** correcting our broken English.

David: Remember the many hours of studying we put in and of burning the midnight oil?

Ana: **Of course,** I do! How could I forget?

David: We certainly gave it all we've got! We pounded the pavement looking for jobs, worked out the problem of finding housing, went for the driving test . . .

Ana: And passed with flying colors! We simply gave it our best shot and counted on moving ahead.

David: As well as daring *to take a chance* every now and then.

Ana: Yes, when the feeling was right.

David: We're fortunate in other ways, too. We've *made friends* with people around us and *have a good time* with them.

Ana: Well, that's because we've tried to understand their *way of thinking,* and they've tried to understand ours.

David: Ana, we have a lot to be thankful for. I've really become comfortable in our adopted country.

Ana: Yes, David. You're absolutely right. We really do have it made. I'm glad we're part of the United States.

Definitions

to settle down: to remain in one place, to have a home and a job, to lead a routine life

    Do you think you will ever settle down? Do you think you will ever remain in one place?

hard up: in need of basic essentials, desperate

    They are very hard up. They are in need of all basic essentials.

to make ends meet: to live on what one earns, to earn enough money for daily essentials

    With his salary, they can easily make ends meet. They can easily live on what he earns.

for the most part: generally, mostly

    For the most part, they work very hard. Generally, they work very hard.

to come true: to be realized, to become a reality

    My dreams have come true! My dreams have been realized!

to snap out of: to experience a sudden negative to positive change in emotion or attitude

    He finally snapped out of his depression. He suddenly became happier.

to zero in on: to concentrate on, to put a lot of effort into

They zeroed in on learning English. They concentrated on learning English.

of course: naturally, certainly, definitely

Of course, you will learn English! Certainly, you will learn English!

to take a chance: to try something without knowing the results, to do something and hope for success

We'll take a chance on starting the business. We'll start the business and hope for success.

to make friends: to become intimate or close with others, to become good companions, to acquire close acquaintances

Most people like to make friends. Most people like to acquire close acquaintances.

to have a good time: to enjoy oneself

We had a very good time! We enjoyed ourselves very much!

way of thinking: opinion, viewpoint, mental attitude, ideas

I try to understand his way of thinking. I try to understand his viewpoint.

None of these idioms may be separated by the object.

Exercise 1
Answer these questions from the dialogue orally.

1. How have David and Ana finally settled down?
2. As strangers in a new land, did they have their share of being hard up and making ends meet?
3. For the most part, how did they feel?
4. Are their dreams coming true? Explain.
5. What happened once they snapped out of the initial culture shock?
6. What did they zero in on?
7. What does Ana mean when she says that, of course, she remembers burning the midnight oil?
8. When did Ana and David dare to take a chance?
9. With whom did they make friends and have a good time?
10. Why have they tried to understand the way of thinking of the people around them?

Exercise 2
Write the idioms from the dialogue that correspond to the words in parentheses.

1. David and Ana have (found a home and a job) _____

   _____ .

2. They had their share of being (in need of basic essentials) _____

   _____ .

3. Sometimes, they had trouble (living on what they earned) _____

   _____ .

4. (Generally) _____ , they were
   optimistic.

5. Their dreams are (becoming reality) _____ .

6. They (experienced a sudden negative to positive change in emotion)

   _____ the initial culture shock.

7. Ana and David (concentrated on) _____
   studying English.

8. (Certainly) _____ , they wanted to do well.

9. They dared (to try something with unknown results) _____

   _____ .

10. David and Ana (became close companions) _____
    with the people around them.

11. They (enjoy themselves) _____
    with their friends.

12. Ana and David try to understand their (viewpoint) _____

    _____ .

Exercise 3
Answer these questions orally.

1. Have you ever been hard up with little to eat?
2. Have you ever had difficulty making ends meet?
3. When did you snap out of your initial culture shock?
4. How do you feel about living in the United States for the most part?
5. How did you zero in on learning English?
6. Do you take a chance when the feeling is right? How?
7. How do you try to understand the way of thinking of the people around you?
8. Do you make friends easily?
9. How do you have a good time with your friends?
10. When someone asks you if you like the United States, do you answer, "Of course, I do!"? Why?
11. How are your dreams coming true?
12. How have you finally settled down?

Exercise 4
Match the idiom to its definition by writing the letter of the definition on the line next to the idiom number.

1. _____ to make friends   a. desperate

2. _____ to take a chance   b. viewpoint

3. _____ to settle down   c. to become good companions

4. _____ hard up   d. to concentrate on

5. _____ to snap out of   e. to be realized

6. _____ to make ends meet   f. to remain in one place

7. _____ of course   g. to live on what one earns

8. _____ for the most part   h. certainly

9. _____ to zero in on   i. to enjoy oneself

10. _____ to have a good time   j. generally

11. _____ way of thinking   k. to do something and hope for success

12. _____ to come true

l. to experience a negative to positive emotion

Exercise 5
Respond to these statements orally.

1. Name one place where you would like to settle down permanently.
2. Name one way to make ends meet.
3. Name something you have zeroed in on.
4. Name two situations that you have taken a chance on.
5. Give one way to snap out of depression.
6. Give one way to make friends.
7. Give two ways to have a good time with your friends.
8. Give one dream you want to come true.

Exercise 6
Underline the words in parentheses that best correspond to the italicized idioms.

1. How have your dreams *come true?* How have your dreams (been realized, not been realized, never occurred)?
2. We got used to their *way of thinking.* We got used to their (friends, relatives, ideas).
3. We *have a good time* when we're together. We (argue with each other, don't enjoy being together, enjoy ourselves).
4. She *makes friends* with her neighbors. She (rarely talks, becomes close, becomes enemies) with them.
5. *For the most part* they did well. (In general, Always, Hardly ever) they did well.
6. Let's *take a chance* on the business venture. Let's (try it and hope for failure, try it and hope for success, not try it).
7. *Of course,* I will go with you. (Perhaps, Definitely, Probably), I will go with you.

8. How did you *zero in on* getting your work done? How did you (memorize, put effort into, forget about) getting your work done?

9. They work hard *to make ends meet*. They work hard (to be desperate, to earn enough money, to enjoy themselves).

10. The family was *hard up* in the beginning. The family was (in need of money, hardly in need of money, satisfied).

11. She *snapped out of* her pessimism. She (suddenly became more positive, suddenly became more negative, remained pessimistic).

12. Finally, they're *settling down*. Finally, they're (moving around the country, living in one place, leading an unstable life).

Exercise 7
Reread the dialogue. Tell the story in your own words using the idioms.

Exercise 8
Complete the second sentence by substituting idioms for the italicized words.

1. How do you *live on what you earn?*

   How do you _____ ?

2. We *put a lot of effort into* fixing up our home.

   We _____ fixing up our home.

3. *Mostly,* we love the people and the culture.

   _____ , we love the people and the culture.

4. Did you *enjoy yourself?*

   Did you _____ ?

5. *Certainly,* you can do that if you try.

   _____ , you can do that if you try.

6. Do you think we should *try it even though we don't know the results?*

   Do you think we should _____ ?

213

7. They aren't *in need of basic essentials* anymore.

They aren't _____ anymore.

8. He doesn't want to *lead a routine life*.

He doesn't want to _____ .

9. She *suddenly changed in her emotion* of depression.

She _____ her depression.

10. Do you understand my *mental attitude?*

Do you understand my _____ ?

11. Some people *acquire close acquaintances* easily.

Some people _____ easily.

12. Which of your plans has *been realized?*

Which of your plans has _____ ?

Exercise 9
Change these sentences to the possessive by using an apostrophe.

Example: The brother of David traded his car in.

David's brother _____ traded his car in.

1. *The aunt of Ana* took a chance on the lottery.

_____ took a chance on the lottery.

2. *The family of our friend* is making ends meet.

_____ is making ends meet.

3. *The parents of Kim* have settled down in Arizona.

_____ have settled down in Arizona.

4. *The brother of David and Mike* understands our way of thinking.

   _____ understands our way
   of thinking.

5. Of course, we hear *the voices of the children.*

   Of course, we hear _____ .

6. *The students of the dance instructor* have a good time.

   _____ have a good time.

7. *The associates of the businessmen* are, for the most part, getting
   ahead.

   _____ are, for the most part,
   getting ahead.

8. *The children of our neighbors* are making friends with our children.

   _____ are making friends
   with our children.

9. The governor will zero in on *the problems of the community.*

   The governor will zero in on _____ .

10. *The teenage son of my friends* snapped out of his unhappy mood.

    _____ snapped out of his
    unhappy mood.

11. Even *the mother of the princess* was hard up.

    Even _____ was hard up.

12. *The predictions of Ana* are coming true.

    _____ are coming true.

Exercise 10
Complete the idiom phrase in each sentence.

1. We finally settled _____ . We're buying a house in the suburbs of Boston.

2. When you snap _____ _____ your depression, you'll feel much better.

3. They were so hard _____ at first that they couldn't even buy enough clothing for the family.

4. She _____ friends easily. Everywhere she goes she meets people who keep in touch with her.

5. He zeroed _____ _____ learning a new profession as quickly as possible.

6. For the _____ part, they enjoy living in the United States. Sometimes they get homesick, but usually they are happy.

7. They try to make ends _____ , but they don't always earn enough money.

8. Let's have a good _____ . We can go out to dinner and then go dancing.

9. To his _____ of thinking, this is a great place to live. He feels there's plenty of opportunity for everyone.

10. _____ course, I want to go with you! Most definitely!

11. Sometimes, we all need to take a _____ and try something we've never done before.

12. My dreams are finally coming _____ ! What I had thought about for years is finally occurring.

Exercise 11
With a partner, create and perform an interesting, funny, enjoyable dialogue. Use as many idioms from this lesson as possible.

Exercise 12
Write sentences with the idioms given.

1. to settle down

_____

2. to come true

_____

3. of course

_____

4. to snap out of

_____

5. hard up

_____

6. to make ends meet

_____

7. to take a chance

_____

8. to make friends

_____

Exercise 13
Circle the letter of the sentence that corresponds to the idiom used in the numbered sentence.

1. At the age of thirty, he was ready to settle down.
   a. He was ready to travel.
   b. He was ready to get married and stay in one place.
   c. He was ready to leave for an unknown destination.

2. She was hard up emotionally and financially.

   a. She had money and felt secure.

   b. She didn't have money and felt insecure.

   c. She had everything she needed and was happy.

3. For the most part, the people in our company work hard.

   a. Occasionally, people work hard.

   b. Once in a while, people work hard.

   c. Generally, people work hard.

4. We made ends meet by saving and budgeting.

   a. By saving and budgeting, we had enough money for living.

   b. By saving and budgeting, we didn't have enough money for everyday essentials.

   c. By saving and budgeting, we spent all our money.

5. After the hurricane, they zeroed in on rebuilding the city.

   a. They had no desire to rebuild it.

   b. They worked very hard rebuilding it.

   c. They put no effort into rebuilding it.

6. They took a chance and married each other.

   a. They married each other although they weren't sure the marriage would last.

   b. They married each other because they were sure the marriage would last.

   c. They married each other because they were certain the marriage would be a success.

7. Of course, he was determined to finish his education.

   a. Without doubt, he was determined to finish his education.

   b. Probably, he was determined to finish his education.

   c. Unfortunately, he was determined to finish his education.

8. They have a good time wherever they are.

   a. They rarely enjoy themselves.

   b. They always enjoy themselves.

   c. They never enjoy themselves.

9. She told the children to snap out of their foolishness.

   a. She told them to continue being foolish.

   b. She told them she enjoyed their foolishness.

   c. She told them to stop being foolish.

10. They made friends with their neighbors.
    a. They don't know their neighbors.
    b. They don't like their neighbors.
    c. They enjoy their neighbors.
11. To his way of thinking, no one is right.
    a. He has definite opinions.
    b. He doesn't have definite opinions.
    c. He isn't certain of his ideas.
12. When my dreams came true, I was the happiest person in the world.
    a. I got what I've always wanted.
    b. I didn't get anything.
    c. I'm still waiting.

Exercise 14
Use *since, for,* or *ago* in the following sentences.

1. I haven't seen her _____ she got married.

2. He came to this city four years _____ .

3. _____ how long have they lived in California?

4. _____ when have you been working at Dynamic Corporation?

5. They have been planning to enlarge their house _____ some time now.

6. It has been raining _____ yesterday.

7. Five days _____ there was a major hurricane in Florida.

8. _____ he met her, he hasn't talked to another girl.

9. She went on vacation _____ five days.

10. The last time we got together was a week _____ .

11. _____ she was a child, she's been into sports.

12. _____ almost four months, they've been arguing about their problems.

13. The presidential candidates have been discussing their platforms _____ last March.

14. One year _____ , the senator resigned.

15. A president of the United States is elected _____ four years.

16. They went on vacation a week _____ .

17. There hasn't been a major earthquake _____ 1992.

18. _____ some time now, they have been looking forward to their daughter's visit.

19. _____ when have you known about their plans to elope?

20. Ever _____ he became a United States citizen, he's been enjoying his right to vote.

Review of Lessons 11–15

Exercise 1
Write the correct form of the best idiom for each italicized definition.
Use each idiom once.

to take it easy	to settle down
to call up	for the most part
of course	to take turns
to catch (an illness)	burning up
to get together	to make good time
every other	to stand a chance
to rave about	to head up to
hard up	to get through
to put off	to take one's mind off
to map out	to come true

1. They can *travel fast* because there is very little traffic today.

   They can _____ because there is very little
   traffic today.

2. The soldiers will *plan* their strategy before attacking the enemy.

   The soldiers will _____ their strategy before
   attacking the enemy.

3. The two friends *met with each other* for the first time in twenty years!

   The two friends _____ for the first time in
   twenty years!

4. The family hoped *to lead a routine life* in a small farm community.

   The family hoped _____ in a small farm
   community.

5. She *became ill with* the flu and went to the doctor.

   She _____ the flu and went to the doctor.

6. Do you *telephone* your friends before visiting them?

   Do you _____ your friends before visiting them?

7. Because he doesn't *forget* his problems, he's constantly unhappy.

   Because he doesn't _____ his problems, he's constantly unhappy.

8. It's good *to relax* in the evening after working hard all day.

   It's good _____ in the evening after working hard all day.

9. He thought my poem was beautiful, and he *enthusiastically praised* it.

   He thought my poem was beautiful, and he _____ it.

10. Must they attend school? *Naturally,* school is compulsory for all children.

    Must they attend school? _____ , school is compulsory for all children.

11. He *has a possibility* of receiving an exit visa.

    He _____ of receiving an exit visa.

12. She couldn't *pass through* the line at the immigration office because she had forgotten her passport.

    She couldn't _____ the line at the immigration office because she had forgotten her passport.

13. The man was *desperate* and needed help.

    The man was _____ and needed help.

14. I always knew my desires would *be realized!*

    I always knew my desires would _____ !

15. We received our paychecks *every alternate* week, not every week.

    We received our paychecks _____ week, not every week.

16. The child was *hot and feverish* and needed a doctor's care.

    The child was _____ and needed a doctor's care.

17. The committee decided *to delay* the meeting until the following week.

    The committee decided _____ the meeting until the following week.

18. *In general,* they were happy with the decision they had made.

    _____ , they were happy with the decision they had made.

19. The children *alternate* cleaning their room.

    The children _____ cleaning their room.

20. While *going toward* the mountains, our car broke down.

    While _____ the mountains, our car broke down.

Exercise 2
Choose the idiom in parentheses that best completes the sentence.

1. We _____ at the motel early in the evening. (better off, looked forward to, pulled in)

2. After six months, he finally _____ and told her what was happening. (took turns, dropped her a line, made good time)

3. He never _____ doing his homework because he doesn't like school. (feels like, takes a chance, takes turns)

4. They _____ plenty of money for the new venture. (put off, put aside, came up)

5. _____ ! This has been a most exhausting day. (You said it, Of course, Rat race)

6. They're _____ spending their vacation together. (looking forward to, coming true, taking turns)

7. He's _____ from morning until night! (taking care of, on the go, better off)

8. He _____ his grouchy mood when he saw his friend. (snapped out of, took care of, called up)

9. Something _____ with the steering mechanism, and he hit the curb. (made ends meet, pulled in, went wrong)

10. When she's _____ , she goes to bed. (on the go, better off, wiped out)

11. They try _____ by working two jobs. (to take it easy, to have a good time, to make ends meet)

12. The fellow was _____ after he had walked ten miles in the rain. (worn out, back on his feet, on the go)

13. Stay near the telephone. I'll _____ this evening. (break an engagement, give you a ring, drop you a line)

14. They _____ solving their immediate economic problems. (thought twice, snapped out of, zeroed in on)

15. We _____ about spending the weekend alone at a mountain cabin. (headed up to, thought twice, have a good time)

16. I'll call you _____ in the afternoon. (in no time, back on your feet, later on)

17. Let's _____ with each other through letters, phone calls, and visits after you move away. (drop a line, keep in touch, call up)

18. He liked the work he was doing even though it was a _____

_____ . (ages, rat race, time off)

19. _____ , they had made a fortune! (In no
    time at all, Later on, On the go)

20. We _____ when we visited the Grand
    Canyon. (settled down, had a good time, mapped out)

Exercise 3
Write the best idiom for each sentence. Use each idiom once.

on the road	came up
odds and ends	better off
what's the matter	comes down with
took a chance	ways of thinking
ran a temperature	shake hands
break the engagement	back on his feet
spending money	get the show on the road
checked in	take care of
from head to toe	time off
ages	make friends

1. When she has _____ from the factory, she
   likes to relax.

2. Let's _____ and enjoy a
   pleasant day at the shore.

3. Yesterday the child _____ of
   104° F (40° C).

4. They are _____ living in their own house than
   in an apartment.

5. _____ with you? Aren't you feeling well?

6. Something unexpected _____ , and now she's
   unable to go with me.

7. The truck driver has been _____ for many
   hours and is exhausted from driving.

8. When Kim had the flu, she ached _____ .

9. They had so many _____ to do that they were busy all day.

10. The children have so much _____ that they can buy anything they want.

11. You should call and _____ so he will know you're not coming.

12. After the long illness, he is finally _____ again.

13. Who will _____ the family if she works all day?

14. When he _____ at the hotel, he had to write his name and address.

15. Last night he _____ on the lottery and won $1,000!

16. When they move to a new area, they like to meet people and

_____ very quickly.

17. The children hadn't been to a circus for _____ !

18. About twice a year he _____ the flu and has to stay in bed.

19. China and America have two different _____ .

20. Whenever they meet each other, they _____ in greeting.

Appendix of Separable Idioms

Separable idioms, two- or three-word verbs, differ from other idioms in that they may be separated by the object. It must be noted, however, that only if the object is a noun can it be placed either within the idiom (i.e., between the verb and the preposition) or after the idiom. If the object is a pronoun, it can only be placed between the verb and the preposition.

Example: noun object   Let's *call up* Jim.
                                      Let's *call* Jim *up*.
        pronoun object   Let's *call* him *up*.

A list of all separable idioms appearing in the text follows.

Lesson 1
———

Lesson 2
———

Lesson 3
to check out
to drop off
to find out

Lesson 4
to fill out
to pick up

Lesson 5
to back up
to put in
to start up

Lesson 6
to call in
to look over

Lesson 7
to tie up
to trade in
to work out

Lesson 8
to make out
to talk over
to think over
to write out

Lesson 9
to do over
to figure out
to fix up
to put up

Lesson 10
to keep in mind
to pick up
to pick out

Appendix of Separable Idioms

Lesson 11
   to call up

Lesson 12
   ————

Lesson 13
   to put off

Lesson 14
   to map out
   to put aside

Lesson 15
   ————

Answer Key

Lesson 1

Exercise 1
Answers will vary.

Exercise 2
1. by air
2. tired out
3. making out
4. counted on
5. Moving ahead
6. to get through
7. Getting used to
8. have to
9. broken English
10. mixed up
11. which way to turn
12. Little by little

Exercise 3
Answers will vary.

Exercise 4
1. i
2. j
3. h
4. f
5. k
6. e
7. b
8. l
9. g
10. d
11. a
12. c

Exercise 5
Answers will vary.

Exercise 6
1. what to do
2. tolerated
3. very tired
4. accustomed to
5. must
6. anticipated
7. plane
8. perplexed
9. poor
10. do well
11. slowly
12. successful

Exercise 7
Stories will vary.

Exercise 8
1. getting used to
2. broken English
3. mixed up
4. moved ahead
5. which way to turn
6. have to
7. make out
8. counted on
9. Little by little
10. tired out
11. by air
12. got through

Exercise 9
1. will adjust
2. will be
3. will send
4. will count
5. will move
6. will make
7. will improve
8. will get
9. 'll be
10. will have
11. will get
12. will know

Exercise 10
1. out
2. up
3. on
4. to
5. ahead

229

6. out
7. to
8. broken
9. to turn
10. by little
11. through
12. by

Exercise 11
Accounts will vary.

Exercise 12
Sentences will vary.

Exercise 13

1. b	7. b
2. c	8. c
3. a	9. c
4. b	10. b
5. c	11. b
6. a	12. b

Exercise 14
1. from
2. to
3. with
4. into
5. at
6. at
7. at
8. to
9. at
10. in
11. to
12. from
13. with
14. at
15. at

Lesson 2

Exercise 1
Answers will vary.

Exercise 2
1. to get going
2. signed up

3. at the same time
4. give it all they've got
5. in spite of
6. to keep up
7. pay attention
8. take notes
9. burn the midnight oil
10. Take my word
11. have it made
12. set their sights on

Exercise 3
Answers will vary.

Exercise 4

1. k	7. a
2. g	8. j
3. f	9. e
4. h	10. c
5. i	11. l
6. d	12. b

Exercise 5
Answers will vary.

Exercise 6
1. wants
2. start
3. works very hard
4. writes important facts
5. even though there are
6. believed
7. enrolled in
8. get what he wants
9. simultaneously
10. study until late into the night
11. on the same level as
12. listen to the instructor

Exercise 7
Stories will vary.

Exercise 8
1. have it made
2. got going
3. set their sights on
4. sign up
5. at the same time

6. Take his word
7. in spite of
8. to burn the midnight oil
9. take notes
10. to pay attention
11. keep up
12. Give it all you've got

Exercise 9
1. is paying
2. are setting
3. are signing
4. Are . . . burning
5. is hoping
6. are giving
7. is learning
8. are taking
9. are saying
10. is getting
11. Is . . . keeping
12. is . . . taking

Exercise 10
1. attention
2. made
3. word
4. up
5. of
6. I've got
7. notes
8. going
9. up
10. at
11. burn
12. on

Exercise 11
Accounts will vary.

Exercise 12
Sentences will vary.

Exercise 13
1. b   7. c
2. a   8. b
3. b   9. c
4. b   10. a
5. b   11. a
6. b   12. b

Exercise 14
1. with
2. on
3. to
4. of
5. up
6. on
7. up
8. at
9. on
10. up
11. through
12. to
13. to
14. to
15. by

Lesson 3

Exercise 1
Answers will vary.

Exercise 2
1. to make it
2. got what it takes
3. pounding the pavement
4. dropped off
5. At first
6. had a chance
7. tons of
8. checked out
9. stopped in
10. had to offer
11. find out
12. going in for

Exercise 3
Answers will vary.

Exercise 4
1. h   7. b
2. i   8. l
3. k   9. f
4. j   10. g
5. c   11. a
6. d   12. e

Exercise 5
Answers will vary.

Exercise 6
1. In the beginning
2. visit for a short time
3. walked everywhere
4. has a possibility
5. excellent qualifications
6. left
7. many
8. has the qualities
9. discovering
10. Read
11. going to
12. get what I want

Exercise 7
Stories will vary.

Exercise 8
1. make it
2. find out
3. has got what it takes
4. At first
5. check out
6. Stop in
7. Tons of
8. have to offer
9. pound the pavement
10. dropped off
11. have a chance
12. go in for

Exercise 9
1. didn't stop
2. didn't see
3. didn't go
4. didn't have
5. didn't check
6. didn't have
7. didn't drop
8. didn't pound
9. didn't find
10. didn't have
11. Didn't . . . think
12. Didn't . . . make

Exercise 10
1. takes
2. Tons
3. offer
4. out
5. drop
6. pavement
7. At
8. check
9. chance
10. make
11. in
12. in

Exercise 11
Accounts will vary.

Exercise 12
Sentences will vary.

Exercise 13
1. a		7. c
2. c		8. b
3. b		9. b
4. a		10. b
5. b		11. c
6. b		12. c

Exercise 14
1. on
2. at
3. at
4. in
5. at
6. by
7. on
8. to
9. in
10. at
11. in
12. at
13. by
14. by
15. in

Lesson 4

Exercise 1
Answers will vary.

Exercise 2
1. is off
2. plans on
3. to give it his best shot
4. filling out
5. to come to the point
6. catches on
7. up front
8. picked up
9. by heart
10. inside out
11. go-getters
12. to get ahead

Exercise 3
Answers will vary.

Exercise 4
1. h   7. l
2. d   8. g
3. a   9. f
4. k   10. c
5. i   11. j
6. b   12. c

Exercise 5
Answers will vary.

Exercise 6
1. tries his best
2. easily learn
3. wrote information
4. memorized
5. wants to
6. open
7. leave for
8. Say what you mean
9. understand
10. has a strong desire to succeed
11. advanced
12. exceptionally well

Exercise 7
Stories will vary.

Exercise 8
1. by heart
2. go-getter
3. are off
4. plan on
5. to get ahead
6. gave it his best shot
7. picked up
8. fill out
9. comes to the point
10. inside out
11. catches on
12. up front

Exercise 9
1. What
2. Where
3. Who
4. When
5. How
6. Who
7. When
8. What
9. What
10. How
11. What
12. How

Exercise 10
1. ahead
2. by
3. off
4. on
5. inside
6. getter
7. up
8. catch
9. best shot
10. point
11. front
12. out

Exercise 11
Accounts will vary.

Exercise 12
Sentences will vary.

Exercise 13

1.	b	7.	c
2.	a	8.	c
3.	b	9.	c
4.	a	10.	b
5.	a	11.	c
6.	a	12.	c

Exercise 14

1. out
2. on
3. of
4. on
5. to
6. off
7. of
8. up
9. up
10. up
11. out
12. in
13. on
14. out
15. off

Lesson 5

Exercise 1
Answers will vary.

Exercise 2

1. going for
2. put in
3. behind the wheel
4. gone through
5. starting up
6. backing up
7. to look out for
8. road signs
9. taken advantage of
10. road test
11. take her time
12. with flying colors

Exercise 3
Answers will vary.

Exercise 4

1.	d	7.	j
2.	f	8.	k
3.	c	9.	e
4.	l	10.	b
5.	a	11.	g
6.	i	12.	h

Exercise 5
Answers will vary.

Exercise 6

1. doesn't hurry
2. in a reverse direction
3. signals
4. spend
5. demonstrated his driving ability
6. driving
7. try to obtain
8. be careful of
9. exceptionally well
10. attended
11. studied
12. began operating the motor

Exercise 7
Stories will vary.

Exercise 8

1. behind the wheel
2. to start up
3. back up
4. road test
5. took her time
6. put in
7. with flying colors
8. go for
9. go through
10. Take advantage of
11. road signs
12. Look out for

Exercise 9

1. is going to be
2. is going to go
3. is going to take
4. are going to learn
5. is going to like

6. Is ... going to go
7. is going to back
8. are going to try
9. is going to start
10. are ... going to put
11. are going to look
12. are ... going to take

Exercise 10
1. advantage
2. flying
3. out for
4. up
5. up
6. wheel
7. Take
8. road
9. signs
10. for
11. in
12. through

Exercise 11
Accounts will vary.

Exercise 12
Sentences will vary.

Exercise 13
1. c	7. c
2. c	8. b
3. b	9. a
4. c	10. b
5. b	11. a
6. a	12. c

Exercise 14
1. up
2. at
3. in
4. out, through
5. over
6. after
7. for
8. out
9. down on
10. in on

Review of Lessons 1–5

Exercise 1
1. road test
2. tired out
3. made out
4. takes her time
5. took notes
6. plans on
7. has to
8. picked up
9. going through
10. have a chance
11. have what it takes
12. by air
13. with flying colors
14. up front
15. burn the midnight oil
16. giving it his best shot
17. keep up
18. was off
19. Little by little
20. going in for

Exercise 2
1. fill out
2. pounded the pavement
3. made it
4. get used to
5. backed up
6. set her sights on
7. which way to turn
8. has a lot to offer
9. stopped in
10. got through
11. has it made
12. mixed up
13. get going
14. drop off
15. to move ahead
16. inside out
17. put in
18. counting on
19. gave it all she's got
20. found out

Exercise 3
1. signed up

2. Take my word
3. road signs
4. going for
5. At first
6. catch on
7. comes to the point
8. In spite of
9. pay attention
10. look out for
11. by heart
12. at the same time
13. tons of
14. behind the wheel
15. got ahead
16. broken English
17. took advantage of
18. started up
19. Check out
20. go-getter

Lesson 6

Exercise 1
Answers will vary.

Exercise 2
1. going out
2. to eat out
3. to take a break
4. How about
5. top-notch *or* out of this world
6. bends over backwards
7. to call in
8. wait on
9. to look over
10. out of this world *or* top-notch
11. Sounds like
12. as hungry as a horse

Exercise 3
Answers will vary.

Exercise 4
1. e	7. l
2. f	8. j
3. g	9. k *or* a
4. b	10. d
5. a *or* k	11. h
6. i	12. c

Exercise 5
Answers will vary.

Exercise 6
1. excellent
2. at a restaurant
3. very hungry
4. exceptionally good
5. appears
6. serves
7. go to parties
8. by phone
9. read
10. tries hard
11. stops working
12. What do you think of trying

Exercise 7
Stories will vary.

Exercise 8
1. bend over backwards
2. looked over
3. out of this world *or* top-notch
4. top-notch *or* out of this world
5. sounds like
6. called in
7. How about
8. take a break
9. to go out
10. as hungry as a horse
11. eat out
12. waits on

Exercise 9
1. goes, finishes
2. is
3. calls
4. eat, am
5. bend
6. sounds, are
7. take
8. is
9. ask
10. look, order
11. can
12. waits

Exercise 10
1. hungry ... horse

2. out
3. out
4. over
5. in
6. sounds
7. on
8. take
9. out . . . world
10. notch
11. about
12. bend

Exercise 11
Accounts will vary.

Exercise 12
Sentences will vary.

Exercise 13
1. a   7. c
2. c   8. a
3. b   9. a
4. c   10. b
5. a   11. b
6. a   12. c

Exercise 14
1. at
2. around
3. on
4. in
5. off
6. out of
7. through
8. to
9. by
10. up

Lesson 7

Exercise 1
Answers will vary.

Exercise 2
1. on its last legs
2. holding up
3. acts up

4. broke down
5. tied up
6. an arm and a leg
7. up against
8. put money into
9. trade in
10. settle on
11. go over
12. work out

Exercise 3
Answers will vary.

Exercise 4
1. l   7. c
2. d   8. e
3. k   9. a
4. g   10. h
5. j   11. f
6. i   12. b

Exercise 5
Answers will vary.

Exercise 6
1. stopped
2. exchange one for the other
3. decided to buy
4. invested money in its repairs
5. find a solution to
6. in poor condition
7. had to decide
8. continues to function
9. didn't always operate properly
10. stopped operating
11. too much
12. inspected

Exercise 7
Stories will vary.

Exercise 8
1. on its last legs
2. settled on
3. hold up
4. trade in

5. put money into
6. to act up
7. went over
8. work out
9. breaks down
10. up against
11. an arm and a leg
12. tied up

Exercise 9
1. won't break
2. won't settle
3. won't trade
4. won't hold
5. won't . . . be
6. won't act
7. won't . . . put
8. won't work
9. won't go
10. won't cost
11. won't tie
12. won't be

Exercise 10
1. up
2. up
3. in
4. arm . . . leg
5. up
6. down
7. on
8. over
9. up
10. out
11. into
12. legs

Exercise 11
Accounts will vary.

Exercise 12
Sentences will vary.

Exercise 13
1. a   2. c

3. b   8. b
4. c   9. c
5. a   10. a
6. c   11. c
7. c   12. b

Exercise 14
1. a. riding
   b. to ride
2. a. hiking
   b. to hike
3. a. snowing
   b. to snow
4. a. leaving
   b. to leave
5. a. driving
   b. to drive
6. a. working
   b. to work
7. a. being
   b. to be
8. a. living
   b. to live
9. a. studying
   b. to study
10. a. being
   b. to be

Lesson 8

Exercise 1
Answers will vary.

Exercise 2
1. writing out *or* making out
2. making out *or* writing out
3. thought over
4. talked over
5. at length
6. keep on
7. looked into
8. pros and cons

9. doing without
10. made up their minds
11. a good buy
12. getting their money's worth

Exercise 3
Answers will vary.

Exercise 4

1. k	7. b
2. c	8. l *or* f
3. j	9. f *or* l
4. a	10. d
5. g	11. i
6. h	12. e

Exercise 5
Answers will vary.

Exercise 6
1. continue
2. well
3. discussed
4. consider
5. positive and negative
6. makes her own decisions
7. writing
8. write
9. contemplated
10. a lower than usual
11. don't need
12. complete value

Exercise 7
Stories will vary.

Exercise 8
1. a good buy
2. make out *or* write out
3. pros and cons
4. talk over
5. keep on
6. to get your money's worth
7. made up our minds
8. at length

9. thought over
10. to do without
11. looked into
12. writing out *or* making out

Exercise 9
1. She thought her
2. He looked . . . his
3. He will make . . . his
4. She must do
5. Is she writing . . . her
6. Her . . . she doesn't know
7. him
8. He made . . . his
9. She hopes . . . her
10. He didn't get his
11. She talks . . . her
12. Does he have

Exercise 10
1. buy
2. over
3. out
4. on
5. pros
6. out
7. length
8. into
9. without
10. over
11. make up
12. my . . . worth

Exercise 11
Accounts will vary.

Exercise 12
Sentences will vary.

Exercise 13

1. a	7. b
2. c	8. a
3. b	9. b
4. c	10. a
5. b	11. c
6. c	12. a

Exercise 14

1. by herself
2. by myself
3. by themselves
4. by yourselves
5. by ourselves
6. by yourself
7. by himself
8. by himself
9. by themselves
10. by herself

Lesson 9

Exercise 1

Answers will vary.

Exercise 2

1. fixing up *or* doing over
2. about to
3. to do over *or* to fix up
4. come up with *or* to figure out
5. to cut costs
6. put their heads together
7. figure out
8. to go with
9. to put up
10. on his own
11. going on
12. on sale

Exercise 3

Answers will vary.

Exercise 4

1. k   7. g
2. l   8. c
3. b *or* f   9. f *or* b
4. j   10. d
5. i   11. h
6. a   12. e

Exercise 5

Answers will vary.

Exercise 6

1. discussion
2. originated
3. reduce spending
4. a lower than usual
5. harmonize
6. remodel
7. hanging
8. now
9. do it over
10. found a way
11. continued
12. without anybody's help

Exercise 7

Stories will vary.

Exercise 8

1. goes with
2. on sale
3. do over *or* fix up
4. about to
5. to fix up *or* to do over
6. put up
7. on his own
8. put our heads together
9. cut costs
10. going on
11. came up with *or* figured out
12. figured out

Exercise 9

1. Have they cut
2. Did we fix
3. Do they prefer
4. Will David put
5. Can I
6. Did she figure
7. Do they put
8. Has the remodeling project been
9. Is Ana
10. Won't they
11. Would it have gone
12. Did the architect come

240

Exercise 10
1. up
2. on
3. on
4. their . . . together
5. my own
6. with
7. over
8. to
9. out
10. up with
11. up
12. costs

Exercise 11
Accounts will vary.

Exercise 12
Sentences will vary.

Exercise 13

1. b	7. c
2. a	8. b
3. c	9. a
4. c	10. c
5. c	11. c
6. b	12. b

Exercise 14
1. for
   ago
2. ago
   for
3. ago
   for
4. ago
   for
5. for
   ago
6. ago
   for
7. ago
   for
8. ago
   for
9. for
   ago
10. ago
    for

Lesson 10

Exercise 1
Answers will vary.

Exercise 2
1. on the run *or* in a hurry
2. in a hurry *or* on the run
3. in advance
4. to pick up
5. to keep in mind
6. run out
7. running short
8. just about
9. picks out
10. mouth-watering
11. are crazy about
12. to cut down

Exercise 3
Answers will vary.

Exercise 4

1. i	7. k
2. d	8. b *or* c
3. f	9. g
4. j	10. e
5. a	11. l
6. c *or* b	12. h

Exercise 5
Answers will vary.

Exercise 6
1. selected
2. doesn't have enough
3. quickly
4. tasty
5. reduced
6. don't have any
7. almost everything
8. like
9. remember
10. hurries
11. before
12. get

Exercise 7
Stories will vary.

Exercise 8
1. just about
2. in advance of
3. to keep in mind
4. on the run *or* in a hurry
5. are crazy about
6. pick out
7. ran out
8. pick up
9. mouth-watering
10. cut down
11. in a hurry *or* on the run
12. ran short

Exercise 9
1. never pick
2. doesn't pick
3. aren't
4. seldom run
5. rarely plan
6. hasn't learned
7. is seldom
8. never forgets
9. wasn't
10. was hardly
11. didn't run
12. rarely keeps

Exercise 10
1. out
2. hurry
3. about
4. about
5. out
6. in
7. in mind
8. short
9. run
10. up
11. mouth
12. down on

Exercise 11
Accounts will vary.

Exercise 12
Sentences will vary.

Exercise 13
1. b
2. c
3. c
4. c
5. c
6. a
7. c
8. c
9. b
10. a
11. b
12. c

Exercise 14
1. them
2. them
3. us
4. her
5. you
6. him
7. it
8. us
9. you
10. me

Review of Lessons 6–10

Exercise 1
1. putting their heads together
2. going out
3. at length
4. to keep in mind
5. ran short
6. in advance
7. bends over backwards
8. on sale
9. on his last legs
10. take a break
11. acts up
12. out of this world
13. picked up
14. put money into
15. looked into
16. sounds like
17. goes with
18. call in
19. up against
20. How about

Exercise 2
1. made out
2. think over

242

3. got their money's worth
4. top-notch
5. in a hurry
6. a good buy
7. kept on
8. tied up
9. came up with
10. to pick out
11. to talk over
12. settled on
13. figure out
14. did without
15. held up
16. to do over
17. put up
18. went over
19. cut costs
20. work out

Exercise 3
1. about to
2. make up her mind
3. fixed up
4. just about
5. to cut down
6. runs out
7. on the run
8. an arm and a leg
9. mouth-watering
10. waits on
11. on his own
12. to trade in
13. How about
14. broke down
15. writing out
16. crazy about
17. pros and cons
18. as hungry as a horse
19. going on
20. to eat out

Lesson 11

Exercise 1
Answers will vary.

Exercise 2
1. What's the matter

2. wiped out
3. worn out
4. coming down with
5. burning up
6. running a temperature
7. caught
8. from head to toe
9. calls up
10. take it easy
11. be back on his feet
12. in no time at all

Exercise 3
Answers will vary.

Exercise 4
1. g	7. j
2. e	8. l
3. h	9. k
4. i	10. d
5. a	11. f *or* c
6. c *or* f	12. b

Exercise 5
Answers will vary.

Exercise 6
1. rested
2. fatigued
3. recovering
4. Telephone me
5. got
6. very hot
7. Soon
8. What happened to him
9. Her entire body
10. extremely tired
11. have a fever
12. got a cold

Exercise 7
Stories will vary.

Exercise 8
1. wiped out
2. caught *or* came down with
3. came down with *or* caught
4. what's the matter

5. from head to toe
6. worn out
7. burning up
8. back on her feet
9. In no time at all
10. run a temperature
11. called up
12. to take it easy

Exercise 9
1. He's
2. What's
3. He's been
4. She'll be
5. he'd, he'd
6. can't
7. hasn't
8. shouldn't
9. weren't
10. won't
11. Let's
12. He'll

Exercise 10
1. toe
2. up
3. out
4. up
5. temperature
6. back . . . our
7. down
8. out
9. no . . . at
10. matter
11. catches
12. easy

Exercise 11
Accounts will vary.

Exercise 12
Sentences will vary.

Exercise 13
1. c	7. c
2. a	8. a
3. b	9. b
4. c	10. c
5. b	11. c
6. c	12. c

Exercise 14
1. does too
2. don't either
3. don't
4. are too
5. doesn't
6. won't
7. would too
8. will
9. didn't
10. don't either
11. does too
12. would too
13. didn't
14. do
15. do too

Lesson 12

Exercise 1
Answers will vary.

Exercise 2
1. looking forward to
2. on the go
3. to think twice
4. time off
5. taking care of
6. odds and ends
7. head up to
8. rat race
9. You said it
10. take their minds off
11. feel like
12. get the show on the road

Exercise 3
Answers will vary.

Exercise 4
1. c	7. i
2. e	8. d
3. g	9. b
4. j	10. l
5. h	11. f
6. a	12. k

Exercise 5
Answers will vary.

Exercise 6
1. enthusiastic about
2. not having to work
3. deodorant and toothpaste
4. went to
5. very busy
6. completed
7. think carefully
8. a confusing rush
9. want to
10. doesn't think about
11. get going
12. I agree with you

Exercise 7
Stories will vary.

Exercise 8
1. odds and ends
2. on the go
3. get the show on the road
4. time off
5. to take care of
6. rat race
7. take your mind off
8. looking forward to
9. to think twice
10. heading up to
11. You said it
12. feel like

Exercise 9
1. for
2. certainly
3. very much
4. definitely
5. many
6. hard-earned
7. any
8. really
9. hard
10. good
11. quickly
12. slowly

Exercise 10
1. twice
2. ends
3. up to
4. the go
5. show . . . road
6. said
7. mind off
8. race
9. like
10. forward
11. off
12. care

Exercise 11
Accounts will vary.

Exercise 12
Sentences will vary.

Exercise 13
1. a		7. a
2. c		8. b
3. b		9. c
4. a		10. b
5. b		11. c
6. c		12. b

Exercise 14
1. up
2. in
3. up
4. out
5. up
6. on
7. over
8. on
9. up
10. out
11. without
12. out
13. to
14. into
15. in
16. up
17. out
18. of
19. on
20. over

Lesson 13

Exercise 1
Answers will vary.

Exercise 2
1. getting together
2. put . . . off
3. come up
4. to break an engagement
5. keeping in touch
6. taking turns
7. dropping . . . a line
8. every other
9. ages
10. getting through
11. give . . . a ring
12. later on

Exercise 3
Answers will vary.

Exercise 4
1. c
2. f
3. i
4. b
5. g
6. h
7. k
8. e
9. j
10. l
11. d
12. a

Exercise 5
Answers will vary.

Exercise 6
1. write him a short letter
2. later
3. postponed
4. meet each other
5. occurred
6. maintain contact
7. call you
8. reached its destination
9. for a long time
10. alternating Saturdays
11. First one then the other
12. cancelled

Exercise 7
Stories will vary.

Exercise 8
1. drop a line
2. to get through
3. ages
4. keep in touch
5. every other
6. later on
7. gave . . . a ring
8. break the engagement
9. get together
10. came up
11. put off
12. take turns

Exercise 9
1. found
2. broke
3. got, was
4. got, was
5. came, called
6. was
7. kept
8. didn't
9. Did
10. put, could
11. gave
12. dropped

Exercise 10
1. on
2. other
3. in touch
4. line
5. engagement
6. together
7. up
8. off
9. ages
10. turns
11. through
12. ring

Exercise 11
Accounts will vary.

Exercise 12
Sentences will vary.

Exercise 13

1. a		7. c
2. b		8. a
3. c		9. b
4. b		10. b
5. a		11. a
6. a		12. a

Exercise 14

1. for
   since
2. since
   for
3. for
   since
4. for
   since
5. for
   since
6. since
   for
7. since
   for
8. since
   for
9. since
   for
10. for
    since

Lesson 14

Exercise 1
Answers will vary.

Exercise 2

1. mapping out
2. rave about
3. put aside
4. spending money
5. go wrong
6. better off
7. make good time
8. on the road
9. pull in
10. check in
11. stand a chance
12. shake hands

Exercise 3
Answers will vary.

Exercise 4

1. k		7. l
2. j		8. d
3. i		9. e
4. c		10. g
5. h		11. b
6. f		12. a

Exercise 5
Answers will vary.

Exercise 6

1. themselves
2. in an improved environment
3. bad things might occur
4. was excited about
5. planned
6. might
7. clasp right hands in greeting
8. signed their names
9. arrived
10. traveling
11. saved
12. traveled quickly

Exercise 7
Stories will vary.

Exercise 8

1. map out
2. better off
3. made good time
4. shake hands
5. stands a chance
6. put aside
7. spending money
8. rave about
9. went wrong
10. check in
11. on the road
12. pull in

Exercise 9

1. is raving

2. will be
3. will map
4. gave
5. pulled, had had
6. checked
7. shake, meet
8. is making, is traveling
9. stood
10. will put
11. went
12. will be

Exercise 10
1. out
2. wrong
3. off
4. good
5. aside
6. on
7. in
8. shaking
9. stand
10. about
11. spending
12. in

Exercise 11
Accounts will vary.

Exercise 12
Sentences will vary.

Exercise 13

1. b	7. b
2. c	8. a
3. b	9. a
4. b	10. a
5. c	11. b
6. c	12. c

Exercise 14
1. for
2. of
3. at
4. off
5. up
6. for
7. out of

8. up
9. up
10. in, at
11. on
12. with
13. down on
14. on
15. At

Lesson 15

Exercise 1
Answers will vary.

Exercise 2
1. settled down
2. hard up
3. making ends meet
4. For the most part
5. coming true
6. snapped out of
7. zeroed in on
8. Of course
9. to take a chance
10. made friends
11. have a good time
12. way of thinking

Exercise 3
Answers will vary.

Exercise 4

1. c	7. h
2. k	8. j
3. f	9. d
4. a	10. i
5. l	11. b
6. g	12. e

Exercise 5
Answers will vary.

Exercise 6
1. been realized
2. ideas
3. enjoy ourselves
4. becomes close

5. In general
6. try it and hope for success
7. Definitely
8. put effort into
9. to earn enough money
10. in need of money
11. suddenly became more positive
12. living in one place

Exercise 7
Stories will vary.

Exercise 8
1. make ends meet
2. zeroed in on
3. For the most part
4. have a good time
5. Of course
6. take a chance
7. hard up
8. to settle down
9. snapped out of
10. way of thinking
11. make friends
12. come true

Exercise 9
1. Ana's aunt
2. Our friend's family
3. Kim's parents
4. David and Mike's brother
5. the children's voices
6. The dance instructor's students
7. The businessmen's associates
8. Our neighbors' children
9. the community's problems
10. My friends' teenage son
11. the princess's mother
12. Ana's predictions

Exercise 10
1. down
2. out of
3. up
4. makes
5. in on
6. most
7. meet

8. time
9. way
10. Of
11. chance
12. true

Exercise 11
Accounts will vary.

Exercise 12
Sentences will vary.

Exercise 13
1. b
2. b
3. c
4. a
5. b
6. a
7. a
8. b
9. c
10. c
11. a
12. a

Exercise 14
1. since
2. ago
3. For
4. Since
5. for
6. since
7. ago
8. Since
9. for
10. ago
11. Since
12. For
13. since
14. ago
15. for
16. ago
17. since
18. For
19. Since
20. since

Review of Lessons 11–15

Exercise 1
1. make good time
2. map out

3. got together
4. to settle down
5. caught
6. call up
7. take his mind off
8. to take it easy
9. raved about
10. Of course
11. stands a chance
12. get through
13. hard up
14. come true
15. every other
16. burning up
17. to put off
18. For the most part
19. take turns
20. heading up to

Exercise 2
1. pulled in
2. dropped her a line
3. feels like
4. put aside
5. You said it
6. looking forward to
7. on the go
8. snapped out of
9. went wrong
10. wiped out
11. to make ends meet

12. worn out
13. give you a ring
14. zeroed in on
15. thought twice
16. later on
17. keep in touch
18. rat race
19. In no time at all
20. had a good time

Exercise 3
1. time off
2. get the show on the road
3. ran a temperature
4. better off
5. What's the matter
6. came up
7. on the road
8. from head to toe
9. odds and ends
10. spending money
11. break the engagement
12. back on his feet
13. take care of
14. checked in
15. took a chance
16. make friends
17. ages
18. comes down with
19. ways of thinking
20. shake hands

Index to Idioms

An asterisk (*) indicates that the idiom may be separated by the object.